D1427478

LITTLE STORIES
FROM THE POLICE COURTS

This book is dedicated to
Sandy Mitchell 1906-1990. Writer. Genius.

LITTLE STORIES
FROM THE POLICE COURTS

ISBN 978-1-84535-807-5

First published in Great Britain in 2020 by DC Thomson
& Co., Ltd., Meadowside, Dundee, DD1 1DD
Copyright © DC Thomson & Co., Limited.

Visit **www.dcthomsonshop.co.uk** to purchase this book.

Or Freephone 0800 318 846 / Overseas customers
call +44 1382 575580

Typeset & internal design by Steve Finan.
Contact: sfinan@dctmedia.co.uk

Cover design by Leon Strachan.

Sandy Mitchell. Writer

LITTLE Stories from the Police Courts has a long and glorious history.

It was a feature that ran in The Weekly News for several decades, from the mid-1950s. Two "cases" were related every week. The idea was that real court cases would be taken, enhanced, fleshed out, given some added "patter" and played for laughs. They were, frankly, comic genius. They deserve to be resurrected.

The writer was a giant of Scottish comedy writing, Sandy Mitchell.

Sandy was born in 1906, retired in 1971 and died in 1990. In between, diamonds and pearls dripped from his pen. He was a staff writer, and rose to be an editor, with The Weekly News and The Sunday Post in Glasgow.

But, quite apart from being a gifted journalist, he also wrote comedy scripts.

He wrote for the likes of Dick Emery, Francie and Josie sketches for Rikki Fulton and Jack Milroy, and (most famously) Parliamo Glagow scripts and books. Stanley Baxter, who so memorably brought those Parliamo Glasgow scripts to life on television, would speak in glowing terms of Sandy as a friend and as an unfailingly polite and kind gentleman. Stanley also pointed out that a superb mastery of the English language was needed, just as much as a keen ear for the Glasgow argot, for Parliamo Glasgow to succeed.

This book is intended as a tribute to Sandy Mitchell, genius.

The Words

THESE are Glasgow stories about Glasgow people who spoke in Glaswegian. It is the purest, most expressive, and best, of the many dialects, accent families, argots (whatever description satisfies your particular standpoint) that are spoken on the British Isles.

Sandy knew everything there was to know about Glaswegian, and English. His insightful grasp of language is the reason that these stories "work" as comedy.

It takes a gifted writer to paint stature, looks, personality and life history in just three or four words. Yet that is what is done in these stories. Sandy had a secret, though. It was that he was intimately aware of his audience. And he knew that people reading his Little Stories would recognise the type of people he was weaving stories around. Their like walked the Glasgow streets, drank in the corner pubs and went winchin' at the local dance halls.

Sandy can describe one person but encompass thousands who were similar. His genius was knowing how to show that those thousand different characters could be seen through the lens of his one character. It was the quality of his writing that allowed him to do that.

In a pale mimicry of Sandy Mitchell's genius, I have attempted to translate some of the colourful, expressive, florid speech into the common tongue — Anglish, I have called it, as I feel "English" doesn't quite cover the fact that even other parts of Scotland might need, and smile a little at, the explanations of Glaswegian terminology.

In any case, "English" sounds like the language somehow belongs to England which strikes me as a wholly inadequate idea of ownership when it is being used best, and most expressively, by Scottish tongues, and by writers like Sandy.

The Violence

IT was a different era. None of the Little Stories in this book tell of thefts, traffic violations, or any of the other misdemeanours that would come before a Glasgow court. They are all crimes of minor violence. No lasting damage appears to be done.

In all cases, the assaults are punished. There is never any mystery about who did what, or denial of the facts given in court. The crimes are owned up to and the guilty are dealt with in a manner consistent with the times.

Sometimes it will be two men fighting, sometimes two women. A lot of the violence consists of various clunks, thwunks and belts perpetrated by women on men. And some of these tales tell of violence done by a man to a woman.

It would have been easy to go through the stories (there are thousands to choose from) and just not select any male-on-female assaults. But throughout the selection process I remained aware that by keeping such tales in there was a danger of trivialising violence against women. Modern society has, not before time, come to revile such assaults. It is a measure of how the world has changed.

However, if I had missed out stories on the basis of gender, then this would not be a true representation of what the Little Stories From The Police Courts consisted of, and what society was like when they were written. I would have sanitised a piece of history when I do not have the right to do so.

I cannot change what happened in the past. I can't ignore the fact that these stories were printed. And no one can pretend that such things didn't happen.

No lessons will be learned if the difficult bits are airbrushed out of history.

Steve Finan 2020

LITTLE STORIES
FROM THE POLICE COURTS

Big Joan's flittin' gies the furnitur' critics a field day

THE great day had arrived – the day of Big Joan's removal to a new house in the suburbs. The word went round the street like wildfire. On all sides was heard the proclamation – "It's a flittin'!"

Soon almost every window had its quota of spectators.

Seated at an open window a few feet above the removal van were Big Joan's next door neighbour, Lizzie, and her friend, Wee Elsie.

They watched the proceedings with great interest.

"Wid ye look at that!" exclaimed Lizzie as the removal men brought out a somewhat well-worn chest of drawers. "She bought that oan the H.P. when she got married, an' she huzny feenished peyin' fur it yit."

Big Joan then hove into view to superintend the loading operations. She directed a fierce glare at the two spectators. "Perra nosey nyucks!" she called up to them. "Ah'll be gled tae wipe the dust o' this place aff ma feet!"

"Better if ye'd wipe some o' the dust aff yer aul' furnitur'," retorted Lizzie. "It dizny look like a flittin' at a'. It's merr like a firewid facturry sellin' aff."

"Away an' clean up that midden o' a hoose o' yours!" shouted Big Joan. "Nae wunner ye've only wan freen', that wee scunner beside ye.

"The only wan that visits yer hoose reg'lar is the saniturry inspector. An' it's made him white-heidit."

At that moment the removal men appeared with a large settee. "Therr the couch she dosses doon oan when she's too puggle't tae go tae hur scratchur!" shrilled Wee Elsie.

"Lissen tae who's talkin' aboot gettin' puggle't!" cried Big Joan scornfully. "Look at hur therr – the Princess o' the Pawnshope! She'd pawn the simmit aff hur man's back fur a slug o' the mammy mine."

Wee Elsie denied that she was partial to a glass of wine.

"You've been merr times at the pawn than ever AH've been!" she declared.

"Away ye go!" roared Big Joan. "Ah've saw ye pittin' yer

furnitur' an' oarnymints up the spout. When YOU look inty the pawnshope windae, it's like lookin' inty yer front room!"

"Don't boather aboot hur," Lizzie counselled her small friend. "She's as iggerent as they make them."

"She's no' gonny insult me!" screeched Wee Elsie. "Ah'm no feart fur hur, big an a' as she is. Ah'm gaun' doon tae pit the hems oan hur!"

She hastened from the house to do battle. When she got to the street she found Big Joan busy helping the removal men.

"Heh!" cried the small lady. "Ah want an apoaligy from you!" Big Joan turned round. "Oh, it's you," she said. "Ah'm gled ye came doon."

Then she retrieved a large, rolled-up rug from the van and, using it as a bludgeon, gave Wee Elsie a drubbing over the head and face.

The screeches of the contestants and the shouts of the onlookers brought the police to the scene. Soon Big Joan and Wee Elsie were being charged with disorderly conduct.

In court Wee Elsie wept copiously. "Aw turn aff the waterworks!" snarled Big Joan.

They were still growling epithets at one another when the magistrate requested £3 from each.

■ **Midden o' a hoose**. A deadly insult. A midden was the place where refuse was dumped. Housewives of the 1950s prided themselves on cleanliness, the sign of a good home. There was even fierce competition over who could best clean the close when it was their turn.

■ **Scratchur**. Bed. Originally a straw-mattress in a lodging house, assumed to be riddled with biting bugs that would make anyone unable to sleep for scratching themselves. Again, an accusation of a dirty, vermin-ridden house.

■ **Puggle't**. Puggled. One definition signifies extreme tiredness, but Wee Elsie uses a secondary meaning – very drunk.

■ **Pawn the simmit aff hur man's back**. Regularly pawn even the meanest of possessions, such as an undergarment, for a few pennies. The insinuation is of living hand-to-mouth, in a very straitened household, and probably a measure taken to raise money for "mother mine" (rhyming slang for wine).

■ **Oarnymints up the spout**. Ornaments residing in the pawn shop.

Eddie goes tae a 'way-oot' pairty – an' gets flung oot

IT was one of those "way-out" parties. The hosts were a with-it young couple, Ian and Lesley.

Sheila was tremendously impressed by the goings-on.

However, her boy friend, Eddie, was definitely not thrilled at all. "Don't tell me we're no' getting' a hauf," he growled as they sat on cushions in a corner of the lounge.

"They're dishin' oot nuthin' but scud!"

"Scud'?" said Sheila, shocked. "What a name to give Beaujolais! Don't you realise it's a wine and cheese party? It's the 'in' thing to drink Beaujolais at parties now."

"Ah'm no' pittin' nae mair o' this beaujolly intae ME," Eddie informed her. "It's as wersh as vinegar. An' that cheese smells tae high hivvin."

"It's Camembert," pointed out the more sophisticated Sheila.

"Well, it looks mair liker ancient cheese tae me," said Eddie. "An' if Ah eat ony mair o' it wi' this scud Ah'm gonny huv the black bile."

The far-out guests were reclining about the floor listening intently to some far-out comedy on record by a far-out American comedian.

It could have been Greek as far as Eddie was concerned. "Whit's this a' aboot?" he asked, bewildered.

"Shshsh!" shushed Sheila.

"Whit aboot beatin' it oota here?" Eddie suggested.

"Don't be ridiculous!" Sheila whispered back furiously. "It's very kind of Ian and Lesley asking us to their party."

"Some perty!" growled the unwilling guest, glaring across at his hostess, Lesley. In a gold lame trouser suit, she was reclining languorously on a divan.

When the comedy record ended and the sophisticated guests laughed uproariously, the hostess called to her husband. "Ian, darling! Supper!"

"Yes, darling!" Ian, a willowy young gent in light blue jeans, called back. "Ai'm just going to prepare it!" And he vanished into the kitchen.

"In the name o' hivvin!" Eddie exclaimed. "Don't tell me HE'S gonny make the supper?"

"Ian's a marvellous cook," Sheila assured him earnestly. "He's gone off to make shish-kebab and we're having that with Turkish coffee."

"Oan tap o' that chape scud an' the mouldy cheese?" exclaimed Eddie. "Nutt fur ME! Ah've hud enough o' society fur wan night. Ah'm getting' oota here!"

They argued for a while in low, fierce tones.

Then Eddie rose from his cushion. "Ah'm fur away," he announced. "Ah'm no' waitin' till Big Jessie comes back tae poison me wi' his Far Eastern muck!"

Just then, Ian reappeared with his culinary masterpiece in a large flat dish. "Shish-kebab, everybody!" he announced blithely.

"Shish-kebab yersel', ya mug ye!" said Eddie.

"What's this fellow talking about?" asked Ian. Then, to his wife, Lesley, he said "Ai'd an idea that this individual didn't quite fit in with the company."

A moment later Eddie dug his hand into the dish, and slapped a goodly portion of shish-kebab over his host's countenance.

General pandemonium ensued.

The police were called after neighbours became concerned by the noise.

Next day in court, Eddie admitted a charge of assault.

"It wiz the scud that made me dae it," he said in mitigation. However, his antics at the posh party cost him £4.

■ **Wersh**. (of food or drink) bitter, harsh in taste, unpalatable. There is no single Anglish word that fully captures the meaning of wersh.

■ **Scud**. There are several meanings. Scud could be a physical blow, a state of nudity, to move quickly, a turn at doing something (a shottie or a go). In this instance, chape scud means cheap alcoholic drink, a wine.

■ **The black bile**. A level of physical sickness that reduces the body to retching until there is nothing but bile left in the stomach. May also be "the dreh boak".

■ **Big Jessie**. Said of a man not displaying traditional (of the time) manly qualities. The man does not necessarily have to be tall or well-built, the "big" refers to the degree of unmanliness, such as being sent to prepare the food. Clearly a woman's job.

■ **Ya mug ye**. You fool. A common and quite vitriolic insult. It means pretentious, easily taken in by new fads, liable to part with money for little return, not worldy wise. The final "ye" further personalises the insult.

Rita's capers bring in the New Year wi' a bang

THERE was even more excitement than usual in the Okeydokey Club when Fred and his Band of Boogie Woogie Bachles discoursed the impressive fanfare that heralded the appearance of Wee Andy, M.C.

As the eager throng milled round the front of the band platform, they held in their hands numbered tickets that had been issued to them as they paid for admission to the Grand Lucky New Year Carnival Dance.

The expression on the face of the Master of Ceremonies was especially benign.

"Ladies and gents," he began. "I trust that each and every one of youse have been gave a ticket with a number thereupon it. On certing of them tickets is a lucky number. Now, the holders of them tickets will be the reciputents of magnificent prizes. So, without no furder procastronation, the lucky numbers will now be drew by me from the box you see fornent me."

The draw began at once. One young lady received a compact. A gent was handed a packet of ten cigarettes.

Big Ella, a large damsel, found herself the winner of a remarkably small headscarf. "That'll never cover hur big bawheid," came the loud comment from Rita the Critic.

"Ah'll cover that big mooth o' yours wi' ma haun'!" called the outsized young lady.

"Ladies! Ladies!" cried Wee Andy in shocked tones. "Kindly do not forget to remember that the season of goodwill isn't not yet terminiated. Do not let us have no more adiposity."

The draw proceeded, Rita looking on somewhat grimly as her number failed to come up. Suddenly the Master of Ceremonies beamed with increased pleasure. "For the holder of THIS number," he exclaimed, "there is nothing more nor less than this handsome bottle of whisky!"

And teetering forward in her long dress to receive the star prize went Barbara the Blonde.

Wee Andy directed his most winning smile on her and, as he handed over the bottle, he modestly lowered his eyes as the blonde kissed him on the cheek.

"It's a dampt disgrace!" declared Rita.

The Master of Ceremonies was mortally offended. "How dare you implicate that this young lady's salutation to me is unproper!" he protested.

"Ah'm talkin' aboot hur getting' that boattle!" Rita cried. "It's a ruddy carve-up!"

"Madam, this is absolutely outrageful!" cried Wee Andy indignantly.

"Aw don't try tae kid us," Rita bawled. "Yiz ur winchin', an' it wiz a cinch she'd get the best prize in yer lucky number swin'le."

Barbara, the elegant blonde, now intervened. "You shut yer big gub," she ordered Rita. "I don't want my afferrs talked about in public".

"By jings, if we talked aboot a' the afferrs YOU'VE hud we'd be here fur two weeks" Rita shrilled.

"If you do not detract these malnutritious allygations, drastic action will be took at once," Wee Andy warned her sternly.

"Ah'll settle hur hash fur hur!" announced the blonde, carefully handing her prize to a friend and marching towards her critic.

"Ladies! Ladies!" cried Wee Andy, hurrying to the scene. "I beg of youse – do not indulge in no unseemly violence, if youse please!"

But Rita's handbag was swinging through the air. It just missed the head of the Master of Ceremonies as he stepped back adroitly, and caught Barbara full on the make-up.

A low emergency whistle was emitted.

Five minutes later Rita was being charged with assault and breach of the peace.

"Ah only gi'ed that blonde bizzim wan scud," she said in court. To her disgust, this solitary scud cost her £3.

■ **Fornent**. In front of.

■ **A ruddy carve-up**. An unfair pre-arrangement of outcome. Guaranteed to outrage fair-minded competitors.

■ **Winchin'**. In a relationship. A working-class, "street" version of courting. It would typically involve dance halls and the imbibing of alcohol in a shared way.

■ **The Boogie-Woogie Bachles**. The semi-mythical Bachles appear sporadically on these pages. Possibly an ambitious nod to The Beatles. One sense of "bachle" is a well-used old slipper, which feeds the second usage (of a person): worn-out, useless, old.

■ **Settle hur hash**. Sort her out, put her right, beat her about the head with a handbag.

A clingin' wee dame has Big Bill bothered

BIG Bill and Wee Frank were congratulating themselves on sticking to their resolution. "Jist think o' it," said the big chap, "we've been oan the wagon noo fur two hale days!"

The glow of virtue replacing their usual type of glow, they made their way to the small dance hall, outside of which they were to meet two young ladies, Lucy and Noreen.

"Ye know, Ah don't know if Ah'll reckanise them," said Big Bill as they waited.

"Nor me, neether," said Wee Frank. "We wiz a bit merry when we chatted them up an' made the date. Ach, but they'll reckanise us."

His prognostication proved correct.

A minute or so later they were hailed with that well-known Glasgow salutation "Hullawrerr!" The young ladies had arrived.

The cronies experienced a feeling of disappointment.

Lucy and Noreen were not quite as glamorous as they had imagined. Not only that, but they were extremely small.

The quartet entered the dance hall.

As the young ladies were disposing of their shiny black raincoats in the cloakroom their appearance was discussed gloomily by their cavaliers.

"Hey, they're hangava wee!" said Big Bill. "Ah know," agreed Wee Frank, "but we never seen them staunnin' up. D'ye no' mind? We sat at thur table an' chaffed them."

"So we did," said the big chap. "But Ah mind you tellin' the Lucy wan that she looked like Elizabeth Taylor."

"Ah tell't hur THAT?" said Wee Frank incredulously. "But her two front teeth are missin'!"

Just then the two small girls reappeared.

Glum-faced, Wee Frank led the way to a table and they all sat down.

To Big Bill's discomfiture, he found Noreen gazing fondly upon him.

"Well?" she said slowly. "Have ye changed yer mind?"

"Whit aboot?" he asked warily.

"Aboot us gaun' steady thegither, of course," Noreen murmured, putting her hand lovingly on his arm.

Big Bill drew his arm away as if her hand were a red-hot poker.

"Ach, they've went a' shy the night!" said Lucy. And turning to Wee Frank, gazing into his eyes, and squeezing his arm affectionately, she gushed, "Ah'm still the only girl in your life, ummn't Ah?"

It was Wee Frank's turn to be alarmed.

Rising so suddenly that he knocked over his chair, he gasped, "Look, ye've goat the wrong idea aboot us! Ye see, when we met yiz, we hud a few refreshmints –"

"Don't boather tae explain!" interrupted Lucy angrily.

"Ah gerrit. Yiz ur jist a coupla patter-merchants that wiz huvvin' us oan."

"An' don't alarm yersels," snapped Noreen, "We're no' that interestit in yiz."

"Thank hivvins fur that!" said Wee Frank fervently – so fervently indeed that Lucy, infuriated by the tone of rejection, aimed a blow at his head.

Big Bill thwarted her in this by giving her a smack on the face.

This cost him £4 in court later. "Ah think it's time Ah went an' hud a snifter," he uttered as he paid up. "It's a deid loss bein' teetotal."

■ **Hullawrerr**. Hello there. A salutation upon meeting that carries a degree of bonhomie and fellow feeling. A person you enjoy the company of would be greeted with a hullawrerr. The person delivering the hullawrerr may have taken drink beforehand, or the hullawrerr might foretell an invitation to drink. There is no fully reciprocal term that catches all the nuances in the less expressive southern Anglish dialects.

■ **Big . . . and Wee.** Friends, and oftime couples, are regularly presented as Big (name) and Wee (name). This is a staple of comedic duos, which provides opportunity for the comedy in itself and also serves to delineate between the two.

■ **Patter-merchants**. Smooth-talking gentlemen, and sometimes ladies, whose intentions and morals are rarely to be trusted and who may well end up disappointed or become the target of violent intent. (Patter is the chat or script such a person would routinely use).

■ **Snifter.** A drink of spirits, served usually as a quarter-gill. Although non-public house measures could be considerably larger. Hopefully.

Coarny coamic John comes a cropper

JOHN was a good-looking young gent, always carefully groomed and immaculately dressed. Susan was thrilled when he asked her out.

"Ah hope he asks me tae go steady wi' him!" she told a friend excitedly.

But soon after they met for the date, the young lady became aware of the harrowing truth about John.

She discovered that the dapper gent was a crushing bore.

At Susan's request he took her for a refreshment to a smart cocktail lounge with pleasant roseate lighting and what she considered to be a romantic atmosphere.

"Ah like the aura o' this place," she said.

"Aura best!" cried the young gent, raising his half-pint of shandy to her, "A' ra best. D'ye gerrit?"

"Aye – but Ah don't want it," murmured Susan, not overly amused by the skilful word-play.

When John eventually controlled his laughter, she said, "Ah see you like your herr long."

As quick as a flash he said, "Ah hud it short, but Ah didnae like it short for long. So Ah let it grow, an' that's the long an' the short o' it!"

"Fancy rat," commented Susan coldly. "Ah could dae wi' anurra vodka."

"Ah'll tell the waitress, an' she'll be rushin' tae get it!" exclaimed her escort . . . to a stony silence

"Aw, ye don't gerrit! She'll be rushin' fur the vodka – Russian vodka! Rushin' ye see?"

"Naw. It's mibbe a wee bit too subtle fur me," the young lady muttered. "Do you aye go on like this makin' ra gags an' whitnutt?"

"Aw aye, ma brain's never still," the wit explained.

"If onybody says sump'n, Ah kin aye twist it inty a joke. It's mah talent."

"Okay," sighed the bored young lady. "Whit aboot takin the bus tae the dancin'?"

John began to laugh. With difficulty he controlled his mirth.

"We – we canny take the bus tae the dancin'!" he choked. "It doesnae dance!"

Susan stared at him even more stonily. "Whit the divvle ur ye bletherin' aboot?" she asked.

John shook his head pityingly at her failure of recognition. "Och, ye're terrible slow," he said.

"You sayed, 'Whit aboot takin' the bus tae the dancin'?' An' then AH sayed – "

"Ach, shut yer bloomin' trap!" interrupted Susan, her patience exhausted. And she reinforced this request by giving him a tremendous thump on the head with her large handbag.

Angry words ensued, and the pair were ejected from the lounge.

The row continued in the street and the police arrived and booked them for breach of the peace.

In court, John tried to explain. "It wiz that Ah hud made a joke," he informed the magistrate. "Ye see, Ah'm a bit o' a punner."

"Ye mean ye're a ruddy scunner!" cried Susan.

The magistrate prevented further dialogue betwixt the two with four devastating words – "Fined £4 each."

■ **A' ra best**. All the best. Good wishes to you, fine fellow/my dear. Might be exclaimed when parting from a friend.

■ **Inty**. Into. Terminology and usage identical to those who pronounce the word differently in their non-Scots (and therefore mostly unintelligible) vernacular.

■ **Whittnutt**. Whatnot. On occasion, depending on context or placement within a sentence, the final consonants can be dropped to produce a voiceless velar fricative – despite their doubled usage here.

■ **Gerrit**. Do you get it? Almost always an un-needed addition to a joke. Might have "Aye" added, as encouragement: Gerrit, aye? if not enough laughter is forthcoming.

■ **Bletherin'**. Talking nonsense, or talking at length. It is a flexible word that can have a very friendly "havin' a blether" meaning. But, used another way, can be akin to an accusation of being a liar.

Hectic hoose-warmin', ends up wi' Betty blazin'

WEE Chrissie was not at all in a good frame of mind at the housewarming party in Betty's new flat.

First of all, she and her boy friend Willie had taken the wrong bus and found themselves lost in the wilds of the East End. They had had to make several inquiries before they eventually discovered Betty's abode.

Then the hostess had received the couple's housewarming gift, a modest tin of biscuits, rather casually.

So Wee Chrissie and Willie sat on a divan looking extremely starchy amidst the prevailing gaiety.

The small girl's temper wasn't improved when Big Isobel and her posh boyfriend, Tom, arrived bearing with them a pair of bookends in the shape of elephants.

"Them is the very things I was needing!" enthused Betty in her best social accent. "I shall pit one on each end of the mantelshelf."

Gently it was explained to her that the miniature elephants were for holding books together.

"Ye'll jist huv tae buy a coupla books. They are things what ye read. If ye can read," observed Wee Chrissie with more than a trace of cynicism.

Her hostess gave her a sharp look. "Whit's up wi' your face?" she asked the small girl. "Ye're sittin' therr as if somebody had stole yer scoane. Fur hivvin's sake huv a drink an' cheer up!"

The refreshments were handed round.

"Hughie gave me them cocktail glasses. Them's are crystal," announced Betty with an affectionate glance at her husband. "They're reelly luvly!"

Wee Chrissie and Willie thought of their small tin of biscuits and looked more glum than ever.

It was then that Betty announced she would regale the company with a song. She stood up and, giving vent to a loud "Ooooh-ooh-ooh," launched into a somewhat shrill rendering of that well-known opus, *Baby Love*.

For the first time since her arrival, Wee Chrissie smiled.

Betty swayed rhythmically, or wobbly, to the song, and the small girl's smile developed into a giggle, Betty's rendition being only loosely akin to The Supremes' highly-polished original.

Soon Wee Chrissie was, in the language of the cognoscenti, "ferr convulsed" and, even though she clapped her hand over her mouth, she could not hide her mirth.

"Baby Love" died on Betty's lips.

"Whit the divvle ur ye laughin' at?" she asked, rounding on Wee Chrissie. The small girl controlled her mirth long enough to cry, "Ah canny help fur laughin' at yer coamic song!"

"Coamic song?" echoed Betty indignantly. "It's no' a coamic song! You're just makin' a fool o' me!"

"Ye're makin' a fool o' yersel'," Wee Chrissie said, getting to her feet. "Ah think it's time Willie an' me went. Ah don't want tae split ma sides laughin' at yer coamic act."

"Dampt perra cadgers!" Betty roared at them as they made for the door. "Ten snifters, six tama'a sangwidges, an' fifteen wee sausage rolls ye've had – a' fur a wee tin o' biscuits. Some hoosewaarmin' present!"

"Oh, we didny know we wiz expectit tae help furnish yer hoose fur ye," said Wee Chrissie. "Next time we come we'll bring ye a hauf-set o' cheeny."

"She dizny need THAT," said Willie. "She's goat plenty mugs here."

The subtle implication was not lost on Betty. With a screech of rage she snatched up the tin of biscuits and brought it down with some velocity on the witty gent's skull. In the scrimmage that ensued Wee Chrissie also received the box of biscuits forcibly on the countenance.

The party ended somewhat abruptly.

In court next day on an assault charge, Betty showed no signs of contrition. "Jist a peety that rotten wee boax o' biscuits hadny been bigger," she growled as she paid her £3 fine, "Ah widda REELLY clonked them."

■ **Tama'a**. Tomato. The word is given a more descriptive timbre by the glottal stop replacing the second T.

■ **Divvle**. The Devil. Auld Nick. The de'il. The beast. Satan. Mephistopheles. The Prince of Darkness. Boris Johnson.

■ **New flat**. This was a time of the great migration from Glasgow inner-city tenements to new-build housing projects.

■ **Perra cadgers**. A pair of cadgers . . . a person who takes without paying, or helps themselves to things they aren't strictly entitled. Not a compliment.

■ **Clonked**. A technical term for an abrupt and heavy impact. The onomatopoeic qualities of the word paint a picture of the event. Affy sair on the heid.

They trusted the fellas to make the punch . . .

ROBBIE gazed with disbelief at his fiancée, Marjorie. "Whit did you say again?" he asked her.

"Ah sayed we're havin' nae boattles o' stuff at the pairty."

Robbie's ears hadn't deceived him. Nae drink? Eh!

But Marjorie went on, "Moira and me's decidit tae huv a big boul of punch an' serve different sorts o' cheese wi' it."

"A boul o' punch?" exclaimed the young gent. "Ah don't fancy THAT! An' neether will Sammy."

"Whit YOU fancy an' whit Moira's fiancé fancies huz nuthin' tae dae wi' it," Marjorie told him firmly. "Moira and me's givin' a punch-an-cheese pairty."

Robbie shook his head sadly. How had his life go so wrong?

He was still wrapped in gloom when Moira arrived, followed by Sammy carrying a suitcase in which were ten bottles of assorted wines.

"You perr kin make the punch," said Marjorie.

The two young gents exchanged a lightning glance in which surprise and pleasure were mingled. With much enthusiasm, they got to work on the punch-making.

After they'd poured a bottle of Yugoslav wine and a bottle of Algerian wine into the bowl, they dipped glasses into the mixture and tasted it. "It's comin' on fine," was Robbie's verdict.

In went two bottles of Spanish sauterne, to further widen the geographical appeal.

Again, there was a careful tasting. "It is nutt too bad at all," said Sammy, enunciating carefully.

Clearly, however, the concoction was lacking home-grown flavours.

But Sammy had an answer for that. "Ah've a hauf-boattle o' whisky in ma poackit," he said. "Ah'll bash it in."

Half an hour later, it was agreed the brew was perfect.

"It'sh – it's goat anough "boady" noo," said Robbie.

The word was a cue for Sammy to break into song. "Gin a boady, meet a boady comin' hru ra rhy," he began to warble in several keys.

Robbie went to his assistance, although the two still touched but rarely on the original tune, and the young ladies, rushing into the room, gaped at them in amazement as the convivial duet went on.

"In the name o' hivvins, they're sloashed!" exclaimed Moira. "How did yiz get like that?"

"AH know!" cried Marjorie angrily, rushing forward to look into the punch bowl. "The boul's no' quarter full, an' the boattles is nearly a' emp'y!"

"Now – now, jusht a minute," said Robbie, gripping the back of a nearby chair to emphasise his point and prevent himself falling over. "Shammy and me had tae tesht the shtuff."

"Thash ri'!" said Sammy,

For no instantly explicable reason, he then began to do a little dance, accompanying himself with a new foray into the world of song which began, "I feel fine –"

"Aw, shut yer stupid big gub!" yelled Moira in a towering rage. Lifting the almost empty punch bowl, she bounced it off her intended's cranium with a resounding clunk.

It was, perhaps, a harder blow than she intended, and Sammy had to receive medical attention. He was, however, as polite (or as polite as was possible under the circumstances) to the attending ambulancemen, inviting them to join him in song while fending off their attempts to see to his head wound.

Thus the assault came to light, and the young lady was charged.

In court, Moira shamefacedly pleaded guilty. On being admonished, she hurried from the dock to join Sammy, who was smiling at her and apparently none the worse for the corrective action with the punch bowl.

■ **Thash ri'.** That's right. All is well. A double translation may be required here from the language of drunken-ness, through Scots, to southern Anglish.

■ **Gin a boady, meet a boady comin' hru ra rhy**. Again, a complicated route must be taken from the original Robert Burns poem to Anglish, taking cognisance of the possibly lethal contents of the punch-bowl on the way. The esteemed Mr Burns was talking about the social responsibilities on the occasion: "If some young gent should perhaps meet a young lady walking through a field of rye". The poem further advises that if the young man should stop to kiss the young lady in the rye field, then she and he might then have to consider themselves a couple. But the subtle relationship nuances of this were probably not germane to Sammy's performance at the time.

Eavesdroppin' Jacqui gets an earful

JACQUI had never before seen the two red-haired young ladies, Kay and Louise, who shared her table in the small cafe.

And it became obvious that the redheads had never seen HER before. For they began to discuss Alan, Jacqui's current boy friend. "Oh, that Alan fella's a smooth operator!" declared Kay. "He took me oot … an' then he took me in."

"How 'rat?" inquired Louise. "Well, we set oot in his car fur a drive inty the country, an' here, did the car no' go and stoap sudden-like," the young lady revealed.

"Aw, Ah've met THAT kina chancer!" said Louise. "He'd tell ye the car hud ran oota petrol."

"Aye, but the car HUD ran oota petrol," revealed Kay. "An' Ah hud tae help him push it hauf a mile tae a garridge. Then Ah hud tae loan him five bob for petrol. He'd left his wallet in anurra suit, he sayed."

Did ye get yer five boab back?" queried Louise.

"Did Ah WHIT!" exclaimed Kay. "Ah huvny clapped eyes oan him since!"

"It's his brurra-in-law's car," Louise revealed. "He gets a len' o' it occasionally."

This disclosure confirmed to Jacqui that the young gent under discussion was definitely her boy friend, Alan.

She squirmed with resentment. "Oh, he's as swave as they make them," Louise went on. "Fancies hissel' as a kina James Bond. Mind ye, ye're apt tae be took in by the rid satin linin' tae his jaicket an' him aye smokin' American cigarettes an' 'rat."

"Aye," Louise said, "Who's the mug he's goat in tow noo?"

"Oh they tell me it's an emp'y-heidit wee blonde he met at the dancin'," Kay informed her.

"She's been gaun' aboot sayin' she's getting' engaged tae a timber merchant."

"Timber merchant?" exclaimed Louise, "She'll get the shoak o' her life when she finds oot he sells bundles o' firewid fur a livin'! Somebody should tell hur how he chaffed Big Millie inty getting' engaged tae him. Then she sent him back the engagement ring in a wee parcel marked 'Glass – With Care'."

"Well, it seems he's goat haud o' a right mug noo," said Kay.

Jacqui had heard enough. "Thanks fur the coampliment," she snapped as she rose. "It's very nice hearin' yerself' discussed by a perra poison-tongued middens, Ah must say."

"Oh, it's Cassynova Alan's latest mug!" cried Louise.

"D'ye know whit's wrang wi' youse perr?" Jacqui said. "Yiz are ett up wi' jealousy. Alan huz tell't me a' aboot youse – the perra ugly big ridheids he took oot in his car oota peety, because nae urra fella wid look at them."

"He's a rotten lyin' nyuck!" shouted Kay, scrambling to her feet in a fury. "He didny take ME oot oota peety. He knowed Ah'd won fower quid oan a hoarse an' waantit tae scounge it aff me."

"He'll go oot wi' onybody tae get money aff them," Louise said to Jacqui.

"Even a pasty-faced wee skeleton like you. Yer big nose an' yer skelly eyes'll no' boather him as long as he kin tap ye fur a doallur."

The candid assessment of her physical features somewhat infuriated Jacqui. "Nae wonder Alan described youse tae me as a coupla dauds o' scruff," she fired.

Further lurid statements filled the air, and eventually Jacqui made the redheads redder-headed than ever by shaking a bottle of tomato ketchup over their respective coiffures.

The undignified scene was brought to a close when the police intervened and booked Jacqui for assault.

"This is whar Ah land fur talkin' tae a coupa ugly female hooligans," she said in court as she paid her £3 fine.

■ **Skelly eyes**. A squint: eyes which do not properly align when looking at an object (strabismus).

■ **Oota peety**. Out of pity.

■ **Gets a len' o' it**. Is given a loan of the motor vehicle.

■ **Coupla dauds o' scruff**. The literal (and more modern) translation could be "two scruffy people". However, "scruff" in this context can be applied to one person or a group of people and means low-grade worthless characters, riff-raff. "The scruff o' the town" could apply to an entire class of people. A "daud" is a large piece.

■ **Him aye smokin' American cigarettes**. An affectation, as all would agree, adopted by a person of quality. The character of the young man in question may or may not fully meet the wider criteria — depending on whether you agree with the opinion of Jacqui on one side, or Kay and Louise on the other. Take care with your answer if bottles of ketchup are nearby.

John flattens a fan of modern furniture

JOHN was feeling rebellious. "Ach, Ah don't want tae visit that coupla wid-bes!" he told Maisie, his wife. "They aye mak me seek the way they'd pit oan airs when they steyed in the close."

"Look, Ah promised Vince an' Gill we'd come fur supper," said Maisie.

"Besides, Ah'm dyin' tae see their new hoose."

At the modern flat, Gill herself, in gold lame evening trousers, opened the door.

"Oh, good evening!" she said. "Give me your coats and I'll put them in the cloakroom."

And she hung them in a press.

"So that's a cloakroom," muttered John.

"Make yourselfs comfortable," said Vince.

John sat down on an extremely low-set chair, and found his knees were almost touching his chin.

"You've got to get used to them Scandinavian chairs," said Gill. "They're very modern. Vince and me didn't want no old-fashioned furniture in wir new place. It's a' modern décor we have goat noo."

"Oh, aye, it's lovely," said Maisie, not very sure what "décor" meant. "But the painters huv made an awfy mess of the walls," she continued. "Still, they'll probably be a' right wanst they're paper't."

Vince looked at her bleakly.

"Them is what we cry murals," he informed her. "A friend of mines who studied art done them for us. They're what is known as 'impressionistical' paintings."

He busied himself at a side table. "We have gave up drinking whisky an' that," he told his guests. "We prefer wine now. It's much more civilised, you know."

John gaped up at him blankly.

"Do you like hock?" Vince asked him.

"Pottit hough?" said John, mishearing.

"No! No!" said his host impatiently. "HOCK! A German wine. Surely you've heard of hock?"

"The hock glasses are in the display cabinet, dear," said Gill.

Soon John was sitting with a long-stemmed glass containing not much more than two mouthfuls of hock.

Swallowing this in rapid fashion, he torturously leaned forward and tried to put his empty glass on a minute coffee table.

Unfortunately, he misjudged the distance and the hard landing knocked the glass off its long stem.

"Oh, he's broke ma luvly hock glass!" cried Vince. "Ah peyed five bob for that glass!"

"Aw, Ah've hud enough o' this!" said John, struggling to get out of his chair.

As he did so there was a sharp crack.

"He's went an' broke oor cherr nixt –" screeched Vince.

His protestations were cut short, however, by John's hand on his face giving him a sharp shove that made him sit down again quickly. The chair he'd been sitting on gave a sharp crack to mirror the first.

John had to pay the penalty in court next day.

"Fower quid!" he exclaimed disgustedly as he paid his fine. "Ah shoulda broke his neck as well as his gless an' his Scandanivvy cherr!"

■ **Press.** Large cupboard, sometimes shelved, often set back in a recess in the wall. They remain common in Scottish houses, as cupboards do in all houses around the world, but the name "press" has largely been forgotten by all but the more seasoned among us.

■ **A' right wanst they're paper't**. All right after they have been wall-papered. "Paper't" should be said quickly, with a solid T on the end. It has a job-well-done air about it that mere "papered" doesn't capture. A wa' that has been paper't will stay paper't. A papered wall, however, may require to be re-done soon.

■ **It's a' modern décor we have goat noo**. The 1950s and '60s was a time of great social upheaval and there were previously-unheard-of changes in living conditions. Glasgow's notorious slum housing was being ripped down and modern-minded young couples were finding themselves in new abodes and were discovering interior design. Often in the shape of Scandanivvy cherrs.

■ **Hough**. From the Scots word for "shin", potted hough is a delicious cold dish to enjoy alfresco on a picnic, on toast for supper, or (Vince might tell you) as a luxurious starter, sliced osso buco-style, similar to a French confit.

The only baldy man in the ballroom

" **A** H wiz thinkin'," said Big Mac. "Ah think when we've hud a pint or two we should go tae the dancin'."

"The DANCIN'!" exclaimed Wee Jimmy, shocked to the core at this suggestion. "Ye're jokin'! It's nearly fower year since we wiz at the dancin'!"

"Ah know," said Big Mac. "An' that's why we're gonny huv big fat paunches oan us by the time we're thirty-five. We baith need exercise tae ger wur weights doon."

The visit to the dancing establishment was then undertaken.

In the dance hall, Mac quickly found other interests in the shape of a statuesque red-haired lady of indeterminable years and considerable waistline.

Wee Jimmy was left on his own.

Despite Mac's success in harpooning the interest of a lady of similar tastes and poundage to his own self, Jimmy was somewhat abashed to realise that the remainder of the ladies were all quite young compared to him.

However, after gathering a certain amount of Dutch courage to lend him confidence, he had two rebuffs to his polite request, "Furrup?" before a sinuous and sulky-looking brunette acceded to his offer.

She preceded him unenthusiastically to the dance floor, with what might be described as a resigned-to-the-ordeal expression.

"Come here offen?" asked the small gent socially, as they embarked in The Shake.

"Naw," came the blunt retort from the young lady, whose name was Sylvia. "An' Ah'll no' come back, neether."

"How that?" asked Wee Jimmy, although with his attention somewhat focused on his attempts to carry out the fairly complicated gyrations required by The Shake.

"Can ye no' see fur yersel'?" said Sylvia ungraciously. "Thur naebuddy tae dance wi'!"

"But ye'er dancin' wi' ME!" her puzzled partner pointed out, giving up most of the more gymnastic demands of this latest dance craze.

"Dancin'?" asked Sylvia young lady crushingly, looking him

up and down. "Ur you sayin' tae me that you ur supposed tae be dancin'?"

Wee Jimmy, stung by this criticism of his rug-cutting skills, redoubled his Shake movements, adding one or two moves from his memory of seeing a ballroom dancer of renown perform several years previously. He was sure this would be more impressive.

When the number was over Jimmy had the temerity to ask Sylvia if she'd like to dance with him again.

"No thanks, mister," she said, staring bleakly straight ahead of herself.

"But we managed no' bad at it," said the small chap, somewhat in hope.

Sylvia then lost patience. "Look, baldy, Ah'm nutt dancin'!" she told him emphatically.

"BALDY!" gasped Wee Jimmy. "You've nae right tae say that tae me, ya impidint bizzim!"

"An' you've nae right tae come here an' dance at YOUR age!" the sultry Sylvia told him. "Ah don't suppose ye'd huv the nerve tae dae it if ye wizny hauf-jaked.

"Ye want tae gi'e up the booze an' behave yersel', like any other auld-age peenshoner!"

"Auld-age peenshoner?" echoed Wee Jimmy indignantly. And he slapped the young lady's face.

Within 10 seconds, he was out of the dance hall and soon afterward in the hands of the police.

He shook his head sadly when he appeared in court on an assault charge. "It wiz jist ma luck tae fall in wi' a teenage toerag," he said as he stumped up £4.

■ **Furrup**. A superb example of the concise and efficient capabilities of Scots. The full meaning of this word is considerably longer in Anglish: "Are you amenable to the notion of getting up on to the dance floor with me?" Pronounciation guide: the double R should be given sufficient length to properly sound like two Rs.

■ **Bizzim**. Besom, a derogatory term for a troublesome female. The 19th Century, and previous, old Scots definition may denote "woman of loose character" or even "woman of promiscuous character". Therefore, as a borderline swearword it should never be spoken in the presence of one's mother, teacher, or meenister.

Folk singer Cathie strikes a sour note with Rita

THE Okeydokey Club poster bore the bold announcement –
"Special Grand Attraction – Two Terrific Folk-Singing Groups."
Inside the hall, even Wee Andy M.C. betrayed not a little
pleasurable anticipation. "Ladies and Gentlemens," he said –
"Tonight I am pleased for to say that we have with us nothing more
nor less than TWO groups of folk singers.

"First of all will youse give your very best welcomes to those
folk-singing stars – Cathie and the Couthie Craturs!"

Three solemn-faced youths in pullovers, carrying dilapidated
guitars, hove into view. They were joined by Cathie, a defiant-
looking damsel with unkempt long hair and attired in a shapeless
dress that appeared to have been hastily run up from sacking.

The youths strummed and Cathie, face expressionless and
voice extremely thin, embarked on a touching ballad –

"Ma laud has gan across the sea;
Oh, fa will bring him hame tae me?
I lo'e him dear, and ilka day
My he'rt cries oot, "He's gan away
Tae fight for Queen and oor counturee,
Oh, fa will bring him hame tae me?"

It might have been described as a magical musical moment . . .
by a man possessed with a vivid imagination.

However, when the plaintive song ended the harsh voice of Rita
the Critic was heard during the pause where a round of applause
might have been. Though no applause came.

Rita cried, "If Ah wiz her laud Ah'd STEY across the sea! Wid
that no' gi'e ye the boak?"

"Madam, be good enough to remain silent," said Wee Andy
severely. "Kindly permit me for to introduce our next guest star.
Ladies and gentlemens, here is none urrer than that great folk
singer, the one and only Wild Bill McGravie!"

The gentleman who answered to this cognomen looked
anything but wild. He was small, with a straggly beard and
checked shirt. His high-pitched voice was hardly suitable for his
opening number. It went –

"I ran off with a gal one day
Tied to ma hoss – away, away!

She said, "Wild Bill, you-all got me scared,"
But I said, "Don't ee be a-feard.
For though I be strong,
I won't do no wrong
To the gal for who I've all things dared."

As the singer plucked at the strings of his banjo Rita's voice, loaded with scorn, was heard again. "Wid ye take a gander at "Wild Bill"!" she exclaimed. "Fancy that wee nyaff cerryin' a lassie away oan a cuddy! He's hardly goat the strength tae haud up his banjo."

"Ho!" piped up Wild Bill. "Ah didnae come here tae be insultit!"

"This is quite true," said Wee Andy. "Drastical steps will have to be took to see there is no repuatition of said insult."

"Ah'll take the drastical steps!" cried Cathie, pushing forward. "Oh, it's Miss Tin Toansils!" jeered Rita.

"It might interest you tae know Ah've jist hud ma toansils oot tae improve ma singin'," declared Cathie.

"Efter hearin' ye, Ah'd advise ye tae get them back in," said Rita.

At that, Cathie snatched Wild Bill's banjo and swung it at the critical one.

"Ladies! Ladies!" called the Master of Ceremonies, "Pray cease behaving like unlawless gents in a football train!"

He stepped back in the nick of time as Rita seized the banjo and brought it down on Cathie's cranium with a string-twanging thunk that might have been described as the most musical note of the evening so far.

Not a second too soon, the low emergency whistle emitted.

The answering henchmen quickly grabbed Rita, who protested her innocence . . . or at least vindication. "She wantit tae banjo me, didye no see it?" cried Rita as she was escorted to the door.

In court for breach of the peace and assault, she had only three words to say – "Shoo'er o' scruff!" The magistrate fined her £4.

■ **Wee nyaff**. It isn't straightforward to translate into Anglish. A stupid, insignificant or annoying person – there are several definitions there, which have perhaps contradicting qualities. It is an insult and almost always given to people of small stature. But size alone doesn't qualify: you have to know the personality qualities before they can be termed a wee nyaff.

■ **Cuddy**. A horse.

■ **Banjo**. Strike or hit. Confusingly, you could be banjoed by a banjo, but a banjo isn't necessary to banjo someone with. You could banjo them with, for instance, a trumpet or a cello.

Riot at the Okeydokey as Rita picks on a Gladiola

EXCITEMENT filled the air at the Okeydokey Club. It was the night of the "Grand Pop Group Festival" – a battle for honours between Seth Stumor and the Scunners and Gladiola and the Flowerlettes.

The event had been dreamed up by Wee Andy, M.C., who backed Seth and his Stumors, while the young ladies' group, Gladiola and the Flowerlettes, had been backed by Mr Humphy McGuffie, proprietor of the nearby Paradisio dee Dance.

Local bragging rights were at stake.

Wee Andy's voice shook with emotion as he faced the eager throng that crowded round the front of the band platform.

"Ladies and gentlemans," he said – "I will now call upon my colleague, Mr Humphy McGuffie, to eluciadate the pros and cons of this great apochryphal contest."

"A panel o' adjudiciators, a' unpertial, is gonny judge, see?" said Mr McGuffie in his laconic way.

"Scunners group plays first an' Flowerlettes saicint, see?

"Panel gi'es points, an' group wi' maist points is furst, see?"

Five emaciated youths with the conventional long hair and guitars shambled on to the platform. "Oh, wid ye look at that!" came the voice of Rita the Critic. "Five hauf-bile't Tarzans!"

"Kindly do not disturb the artistes at this most vital junctunt in their careers!" Wee Andy warned her.

The Scunners plunged into their first number, Seth Stumor, in a strangled falsetto, singing the deeply-moving words: -

"Ra girl I love has went an' broke my heart;
All of ra time we still remain apa-art.
She treats me 'zif I only was hur brurra,
For she is going steady with anurra –"

"By jings, Ah don't blame hur!" called Rita as the singer paused for breath. "He looks like a mop the mice had goat at."

Mr Humphy McGuffie then introduced his candidates. Gladiola and her accompanying Flowerlettes turned out to be five young ladies with straggly blond hair. They had gone the extra mile, perhaps a mile and a hauf, with their tight-fitting long dresses in black shiny plastic.

"Oh, fur hivvin's sake!" cried Rita. "Whit's this we're getting' noo? Jist look at them! They should cry thursel's the Black Puddens."

Her further animadversions were swamped by a stentorian bellow from Gladiola. She strummed her guitar and roared –

I wanna boy who says that I'm ra tops;
I wanna boy whose luv just never stops;
I wanna boy –

Suddenly Gladiola's voice died away to a whisper, although she mouthed and jigged on. The microphone had gone dead.

"Oh, that's a right blissin'!" exclaimed Rita. "Ma eardrums wiz jist aboot away fur a burton wi' hur shoutin'. Ye canny hear hur ahint a bus ticket noo."

"Stoap! Stoap!" Mr Humphy McGuffie cried to the group. "Somebody's went an' cut aff their electricity."

"Whoever done it should get a medal," Rita declared. "It's a bloomin' imposition peyin' money tae listen tae that big hoatch an' hur stooges!"

"She pit me aff tae begin wi!" screeched Gladiola. "She stertit speakin' the minnit Ah began "Ah Wanna Boy!""

"It's no' a boy you waant, strawheid," Rita told her. "It's a new sound boax. Yiz kin sing hee-haw."

This assessment stung Gladiola. The enraged singer seized the microphone and swung it in the direction of Rita's head.

Wee Andy stepped back in the nick of time. Rita also ducked, but just as quickly stepped back into the fray and gave Gladiola a resounding smack on the face.

In a trice the Master of Ceremonies emitted the low emergency whistle, and the henchmen escorted Rita from the premises.

She betrayed little penitence when she appeared in court on an assault charge. "Ah shoulda steyed in the hoose an' watched Panormania," she said, as she paid her £3 fine.

■ **Song competitions**. The two stories just related refer to singing contests at the Okeydokey Club and denote the various opportunities that such nitespots would offer prospective artistes. Some wonderful, bound-to-be-famous singers got their first break in this manner. But for every great crooner there was a not-so-great crooner.

■ **Strawheid**. A disparaging term for a blonde. Possibly suggesting her hair colouring might have relied on the contents of a bottle.

■ **The low emergency whistle**. This term is often mentioned in accounts of contretemps that take place in the Okeydokey Club. It isn't an easy sound to replicate, but its effectiveness for summoning "muscle" to restrain combatants (one of whom will usually be Rita the Critic) cannot be underestimated.

Party photo session sparks a flash-point

EAGERLY, the young ladies in the cafe crowded round Chrissie to see the photographs her boy friend had taken at the party they'd all attended a few nights before.

"Oh, they've came oot rerr!" announced Chrissie. "Ernie's hangava good wi' that wee camera o' his wi' the flash thing oan it, izze no'."

"That's me bendin' ower tae pit P.J. Proby oan the record-player," she continued.

"Ye coulda fooled me," said Wee Sandra. "It looks like the hin' end o' a double-decker."

"Wherr um Ah?" asked the glamorous Gloria. "Wiz nae photies took o' me at a'?"

"Oh, aye," Chrissie assured her, "Here's wan."

And she displayed a photograph of Gloria happily seated on the knee of a young gent and waving both hands gaily at the camera.

"Wait a meenit. That's Tommy!" exclaimed Big Linda indignantly, recognising the young gent with the accommodating lap as her boy friend.

"Ach, it wiz jist a terr," explained Gloria. "Ernie sayed it wid make a better photy if Ah sat oan Tommy's knee for a saicint."

"Whaur wiz Ah when that photy wiz took?" Big Linda wanted to know.

"Wait tae Ah see," said Chrissie, going through the snaps. "Oh, here ye ur – in the kitchenette waashin' up the dishes. Ye mebbe shoulda took the fag oot yer mooth when ye wiz bein' took."

"Aye, ye've screwed up yer face, an' it's made yer eyes look even merr wee-er than they ur," remarked Gloria.

"Oh, here a good group o' us a'!" said Chrissie hastily. "You look smashin' in it, Linda!"

A few photographs later, however, trouble flared up anew.

Chrissie produced another photograph of Gloria sitting on Tommy's knee. This time the young gent was looking up fondly at the glamour girl, with his arm fairly tightly wound round her waist in case she might overbalance.

She had both of her arms around his neck, clearly for similar safety reasons. And her face was rather close to his, although the reasons for this weren't entirely clear.

"Whaur were ye when THAT yin was took?" asked Wee Sandra cattily.

"Big Blondie here huz ferrly pit the fluence oan yer boy friend, huz she no! He looks cheery."

"Aw, it wiz jist a joke," said Gloria.

Big Linda glared at the photograph.

"Aye, it wiz jist a joke," she agreed. "Tommy aye acts daft when he's hud a bevvy. We better no' let him see that photy. It wid make him feel that stupit."

"Whidd'ye mean by RAT?" Gloria asked her angrily.

"Well," said Big Linda calmly, "The day efter the pairty he sayed tae me, 'Who wiz thoan horse-faced big blondie that wiz aye jumpin' oan tae ma knee the minute you wiz oot the room?'"

A noise not unlike that of a giant jet bomber taking off came from Gloria.

"That's a dampt lie!" she screeched, and she grabbed Linda by the hair and gave her what was later termed by several knowledgeable witnesses as a "hangava wallop oan ra crust."

The police were inevitably called to sort out the resulating stramash and duly took notes on the quality and severity of the aforementioned "wallop".

The administering of the chastisement cost Gloria £3 in court next morning.

■ **Hin' end o' a double-decker**. Hind end of a double-deck bus. A scathing comment on the height and width of a young lady's derrier.

■ **Oan ra crust**. On the head. The head/crust metaphor was often used, and proved quite apt in describing the hard outer shell encasing the doughy inner matter.

■ **Merr wee-er**. More smaller. A tautological phrase, but the merr is intended solely as emphasis. Merr could, for extra effect, have stress placed upon it, with rich attention given to the "rr" to significantly further describe the small size of Big Linda's screwed-up eyes.

■ **Jist a terr**. A tear, a joke. The tear is of the ripping sort, not salt water from the eyes. The terminology is out of date, even in other dialects. It has gone to the great slang graveyard in the sky, buried close to "groovy", "far out" and "daddy-oh".

Big May loses her rag with a home-spun dressmaker

BIG May admired Sandra's dress at the dancing. "Oh, it's awfy well made," she said. "Wherr did ye buy it?"

"It's no' a bought dress," Sandra revealed. "Wee Moira made it. Oh, she's rerr at makin' dresses. She jist came up tae ma hoose, measured me, an' Ah hud it a week later."

The large damsel was greatly impressed.

"Oh, Ah'll huv tae get hur tae make ME wan like that," she said. "Ah need a wee dress that wid dae fur gaun' oot tae dinner in, an' sich-like."

So Wee Moira was commissioned to make the dress. But when she brought it to Big May, she encountered unlooked-for difficulties.

"Oh, Ah don't know if that shade o' rid suits me," complained Big May when she put it on and glared at herself in the wardrobe mirror.

"Is it no an awfy RORY rid?"

"Well, that wiz the colour ye picked yersel'," said Wee Moira patiently.

"Oh, Ah don't know," mused Big May, still examining her reflection. "D'ye think this dress suits ma personality?"

"Oh, aye," said Wee Moira innocently. "It's plain an' simple."

Big May gave her a searching look.

"It's mibbe a bit TOO simple fur me," she said. "D'ye no' think Ah'd need a wee bolly-ro jaickit tae werr wi' it?"

"If ye like," said Wee Moira. "But it wid make ye look merr top-heavier than usual even."

"Whidd'ye mean – 'merr top-heavier'?" asked the large girl in offended tones.

"Well, yer shouthers izny exackly wee," Wee Moira told her. "That's why Ah advised ye tae huv them covered up."

"Ah see," muttered Big May, far from pleased.

She searched for more faults in the dress. "It's no' jist as close-fittin' as Ah thought it wid be," she said, twisting round to obtain a view of her back. "The dress ye made fur Sandra shows aff hur figger."

"Oh, but Sandra's got a neat wee figger," Wee Moira pointed out rather tactlessly.

The implication was not lost on Big May.

"Whit's wrang wi' MA figger that Ah canny werr a tight-fittin' dress?"

The dressmaker pondered briefly. "Well, ye see," she said, "if Ah make that dress ony tighter it's no' gonny hing right. Ye see, the way ye're built at aroon' yer backside wid make it stick oot an' spile the line."

"Ur you insinyatin' that Ah've got a big –" Big May began.

"Ah'd say ye've got a kinna mature figger," Wee Moira told her diplomatically.

Her customer was indignant. "Let me tell you," she cried, "Ah've been tell't that Ah've goat the figger of a girl of sivvinteen!"

"Ye've got the figger of a girl of sivvinteen?" said Wee Moira, losing patience. "Ye'd better gie hur it back quick afore ye get it ony furder oota shape."

"Ye've went an' made an absaloot hash o' this dress!" declared Big May angrily. "Look at it. Apart fae everythin' else, it's faur too long. It covers ma knees!"

"Of course it covers yer knees!" Wee Moira snapped back at her. "Ah wiz daen' ye a favour. Ye shairly don't want tae go aboot showin' thae big knobbly joints o' yours!"

This final observation on her body shape made Big May's face go as red as the dress.

"Impiddent wee getherup!" she screeched, giving the small girl a smack on the face.

In court next morning, she was firmly chastised from the bench, being warned that ill-fitting dresses and vital-statistic discussions should not be taken as an excuse to fashion pain upon others.

She was instructed to disburse £3 for the clouting of the couturiere.

■ **Sivvinteen**. The wonderful Scottish way of saying seventeen, that suggests not just a number, but contains a sprinkling of youthful freshness – and yet also an intonation of credulity that Big May might believe she looked like a 17-year-old.

■ **Absaloot hash**. A complete mess. Again, there is a wealth of meaning that can be injected into the phrase with a Glasgow accent. A level of disdain can be achieved that just wouldn't be possible for anyone born south of Newton Mearns.

Vicky takes exception to her greetin'-faced boyfriend

VICKY had been going around with Robbie for almost two weeks, and, now the first flush of attraction had passed, disillusionment had set in.

"He's aye findin' fault wi' things," she confided to her friend, Ella. "He's never happy like."

"Mibbe he's goat a sair stummick," said Ella. "That wid gi'e him that kinna dour look he huz."

"Ach, Ah'm fed up wi' his greetin' face," Vicky declared. "Ah'm gaun' oot wi' him the night. If he mumps aboot anythin', Ah'm gonny gi'e him the heave."

In the cinema that night, the young gent soon became as censorious as ever. "This fillum's an insult tae the intelligence!" he exclaimed. "In real life a fella wid never say tae a dame that she wiz —"

"Aw, shut yer face an' let's hear whit they're sayin'," snapped Vicky.

Her escort relapsed into sulky silence.

When the film came to an end he sighed loudly, "That's the worstest pictur' Ah've saw fur a long time! Ah don't know whit ye seen tae laugh at in it!"

This served only to further stir Vicky's discontent with him. "Whit ur ye talkin' aboot?" asked the young lady irascibly. "It wiz rerr! Ah enjoyed every saicint o' it! C'moan, we'll go up tae the hoose noo an' play some records."

As soon as they were in the house, the sounds of The Beatles singing Ticket To Ride filled the room.

"'Zat record no' jist faaab!" enthused Vicky when the number was over.

"Ah widny know aboot THAT," said the critical one. "Ah don't know whit 'Ticket Tae Ride' means. In fact, Ah don't know whit it's a' aboot. Can Ah help it if Ah prefer Choppin an' sich-like tae the kinna stuff yer Beatles plays?"

"By jings, you've a nerve critycisin' The Beatles!" exclaimed the young lady.

"It's a wunner ye condescendit tae ask me tae go oot wi' ye!"

"Well, Ah like tae be honest," said Robbie. "An' if ye asked me, I could make some critycism o' you an' a', ye know."

A more intuitive man might have been alarmed by the icy atmosphere that settled over the room.

After a deep breath, Vicky grimly said, "Oh, an' whit huv ye goat tae critycise aboot ME?"

"Well – er – ye're no' mature anough," said her boy friend with reckless candour.

"Whit exackly do you mean by RAT?" asked the young lady, reddening with rage.

"Jist that ye should be thinkin' o' merr seriouser things than daft fillums an' funny TV shows an' pop music an' a' that," stated Robbie.

"Ah'll tell ye this!" cried Vicky. "Ah'm thinkin' o' somethin' serious right noo!"

"Oh, whit's that?" Robbie queried calmly, still not seeing the danger.

"Ah'm thinkin' Ah've been a bloomin' mug for pittin' up wi' your cheek so long!" she yelled. And she gave the critical one a blow on the face with her fist.

The resultant noisy rumpus alarmed the neighbours so much that police were summoned, which set in chain a course of events that culminated charges of breach of the peace being made against both of them.

Their romance finally foundered in court when the magistrate asked them to stump up £3 apiece.

"Ah'm well shoat o' that mallycontent," said Vicky as she stumped up her £3.

■ **He's never happy like.** The addition of "like" on the end of a sentence has several possible meanings, and also no meaning. The "like" can serve to denote multiple occasions, but those occasions do not need to be stated, the "like" invokes them. It may also be merely a verbal crutch, used in the way some people might ad "You know what I mean" on the end of sentences, but not expect a reply.

■ **Dame.** Young ladies are no longer referred to as "dames". It is a label that has gone so far out of fashion it is now regarded as an insult.

■ **It's a wunner.** It's a wonder. Comparing some event to "a wonder" was a common habit.

■ **The Beatles.** A four-piece beat combo who became so popular in the 1960s that criticism of them would immediately set aside a person as a social leper.

Deirdre's high hair-style makes George feel low

EVEN with his Cuban-heeled boots on, Wee George was rather small. So he was well pleased when he managed to secure a series of dates with Deirdre, who was a full half-inch shorter than him – when wearing flat-heeled shoes,

But he received a rude shock when the diminutive damsel appeared at the trysting-place.

To Wee George's eyes, she seemed to have acquired the stature of a giantess. "Whit the divvle's happen't tae YOU?" he exclaimed.

"Whidye mean?" asked the young lady. "Ye mean ma herr? Ah've jist new hud it did. It's whit they cry a French roll."

"It looks merr liker a pan loaf stickin' oan tap o' yer napper," said Wee George.

Then he realised that Deirdre's countenance was at a higher level than his own. "Ah've goat tae look up at yer dial noo," he observed.

"Ah know," said she calmly. "Ah've goat oan ma high heels."

Her cavalier looked down and saw that her shoes had the highest heels he'd ever seen.

"By goash, thur high a' right!" he cried. "Wi' thae heels an' that herr ye look like a haystack on stilts."

"It's you that's that wee," retorted Deirdre. "Ah canny help it if Ah'm tall. Come on, if we're gaun' tae the dancin' we'll huv tae get a taxi!"

With a certain unwillingness, Wee George hailed a taxi. "Right, in ye get," he said to his fair partner, giving her a helping shove.

"Oh, ma herr!" screeched Deirdre, forgetting the height of her coiffure and not bending her head low enough.

"You made me catch it oan the roof! Whit ur ye pushin' me fur?"

They were still not on the best of terms when they got into the small dance hall.

"Ah'll huv tae away an' see whit Ah can dae aboot ma herr," Deirdre told the small gent. "Ye've ruin't it!"

So Wee George hung about looking most disgruntled as his partner glared into a looking glass in the powder room and struggled to get her coiffure back into position.

Close on thirty minutes elapsed before she reappeared.

"Ah've jist managed tae get it up an' nae merr," she said. "Ah'll huv tae go back tae the shop ra mora an' get it relacquer't or sump'n. You made a right hash o' it when ye pushed me inty that taxi!"

Thereafter, with sullen faces, they performed The Shake together. At one point in her convulsions, Deirdre bent her head.

Wee George, who was performing skilful hand movements, simultaneously and inadvertently hit the young lady's extensive hairdo with the palm of his hand.

There was a wild cry of dismay from her as her hirsute skyscraper again came crashing down about her ears. "Oh, ya clumsy wee numbskull ye!" she yelled. "Luk whit ye've went an' did tae ma French roll now!"

"Ach, ye're better wi' yer herr doon, onyway," the small gent told her angrily. "It helps tae hide yer big greetin' face.

"Onyway, that French roll dizny suit onybody that's goat a face like a bap."

For a full second Deirdre stood breathing heavily in speechless rage, then, with a roar, she wrenched off one of her very large shoes and belaboured her candid cavalier over the head with it.

Officials saved Wee George from serious injury, and Deirdre was escorted from the premises.

When she threatened to re-enter the dance hall to "knoack his ruddy heid aff", the police were summoned.

In court on charges of assault and breach of the peace, she was quite composed. But the memory of her disastrous evening clearly rankled. "Hope Ah never see that wee oaddity again," she growled as she disbursed £2.

■ **Ma herr**. My hair. Usually the second word is stressed. The usage of herr, with a rolled "r" is much more expressive than the drawled, almost silent "rr" of southern dialects. Another example of the superiority of Scots.

■ **Napper**. Heid. Head. Napper is used informally and often when a certain level of disrespect or humour is intended. The term may refer to getting your head down/ taking a nap.

■ **Ra mora**. Tomorrow.

■ **Goat a face like a bap**. Got a face like a . . . I can only fall back on the definition given in Jamieson's Scottish Dictionary 1808 — "**Bap**. A roll, a small loaf of wheaten bread of an oblong form." To have one's facial features described in such terms was not a compliment.

Ding-dong over Ernie's missing dentures

SUSAN glanced sharply at her husband Ernie's countenance. "Whit's up wi' yer mooth?" she asked. "It's lookin' awfy clappit-in like."

"Ah huvny goat ma boattom denchur in," he explained. "Ah've goat a wee ulcer oan ma gum, an' it gi'es me gyp when the plate comes against it."

"Hivvins, it makes ye look like an' aul' man when ye've nae boattom teeth in," commented the lady disapprovingly.

"Ye canny go tae Isabel's pairty the night like that."

"Ah'm no' pittin in ma boattom denchurs tae go tae Isabel's pairty!" Ernie told her firmly. "Ah'm no' sufferin' agony fur you nor Isabel nor naebuddy!"

So, not on the best of terms, they set out for Isabel's party in the rather posh suburb.

The hostess gave them her usual genial welcome – "Hullo, youse!"

Then she directed a penetrating glance at Ernie. "Oh, my, you've went awful thin about the face!" she exclaimed.

Leaving the two to glare at each other, she went off to supervise the serving of the buffet supper.

Ernie soon found himself confronted by an attractive young suburbanite who carried a plate with a half cabbage on it.

Into this were stuck numerous cocktail sticks on which were staked (in order) an olive, a piece of cheese and a chunk of pineapple.

"Do trai mai hors d'oeuvres!" she urged.

Extracting one of the loaded little sticks from the cabbage, she thrust it into Ernie's unwilling hand.

Ernie reckoned he might be able to cope with the cheese, feared the pineapple would be difficult, and didn't have a clue about the olive.

However, ever the gentleman and somewhat thankful that he hadn't been expected to eat the cabbage, he took the stick and attempted to ignore the eager-looking lady.

But she wasn't to be dissuaded and again suggested that he try it. "Ai hiv tried this recipe from a magazine," she said. "Do trai it."

Ernie, still not entirely sure if he liked olives, having never eaten one, teeth in or not, made a desperate attempt to bite a small piece out of the unattractive black bud.

However, this proved to be an impossible thing to do with only a top plate. It turned into quite a struggle between Eddie, the olive and his mouth.

Suddenly the olive itself took responsibility and seemed to jump off the stick and into his mouth of its own accord.

With the young lady's eyes still fixed on him in fascination, Eddie tried gamely to chew it. As he did so, the oily olive slid quickly to the back of his throat.

"Glug … glug … glug!" he uttered, bending double and making desperate hand movements towards his throat.

"In the name o' hivvins!" cried Susan, whirling round, "Whit's up wi' you now?"

"Ai do hink he might be choking," the young lady told her.

Susan, a woman of action, immediately gave her husband a tremendous thump on the back.

He put his handkerchief to his mouth. Into it shot not only the remains of the olive, but his top denture.

One of the fashionable young gentlemen present, going by the name of Boaby, saw a humorous side to the contretemps. "Misadventures with his dentures!" he exclaimed with a hearty laugh, the assembled party-goers joining in the mirth.

This was too much for the half-choked and highly embarrassed Ernie.

"Aye. Funny eh? Allow me to shut your big gub fur ye," he responded in polite tones, though with the light of battle clearly shining in his eye.

A moment later the wisecracking young Boaby was reeling across the floor from a straight right to the chin.

The blow led to Ernie's appearance in court next day. Clenching his dentures, he stumped up £4.

■ **Awfy clappit-in like**. Very shrunken or contracted. Not an observation that denotes health or attractiveness.

■ **Do trai mai**. In a departure from our normal glossary direction, we shall translate into the Glaswegian. "Do trai mai" is French for gaun hae wan.

■ **Your big gub.** Your big mouth. The description of size refers to Boaby's propensity to talk, as much as physical dimensions. Gub was a well-used word for mouth, probably coming from the Irish Gaelic "gob", a bird's beak.

Melanie the Mod sends Malky off his rocker

MALCOLM was embarking on that most perilous of undertakings – a blind date.

It had all been arranged by his friend, Dave.

"Ye see, Ah arranged tae take oot ma cousin, Sue," Dave explained. "But she'd furgoat she had tae see hur pal, Melanie. So Ah sayed Ah'd bring YOU along."

"Ah hope this Melanie dame's a looker," said Malcolm as they trudged along the street to the place of assignation.

"It wid be a deid loss if she wiz a wee mousey thing wi' nuthin' tae say fur hursel'."

Ten minutes later, when they foregathered with the two young ladies, Malcolm realised that Melanie was anything but bashful.

She was wearing a strange white shift-like dress that looked like a nightgown, black stockings, green jack-boots, a man's cloth cap, and huge circular sunglasses.

And she responded to his polite "How d'ye do" with a hearty "Hiya, daddy-o!"

Melanie, in fact, was what was known amongst the new intelligentsia as a "mod-bird." So also was her friend Sue, though not quite so mod in her attire.

Malcolm had the feeling, from the way she surveyed him, that Melanie did not altogether approve of his conventional sports jacket and flannels.

"Say, that horse blanket is way out, man! It's a panic, daddy-o!" And she giggled gaily.

"Ah'm gled ma sports jaickit gi'es ye a laugh," said Malcolm huffily. "It's no' hauf as funny-lookin' as that bunnet ye've goat stuck oan yer napper. Mammy-o!"

Sue quickly poured oil on the troubled waters. "Whit about a shot before we take off fur the dancin', mates?" she suggested.

The young gents looked at one another, startled. But a "shot," it appeared, meant nothing more sinister than a refreshment.

So they adjourned to a lounge.

After the "shot" they made their way to a dance hall.

Once inside, Malcolm asked his partner, "Ur ye no' gonny take aff yer bunnet?"

"Man, you're not with it," Melanie informed him. "The headgear is part of the rig. See? Ye jist don't unnerstand kinky gear like ma bunnet an' ma green boots".

"Ye're right therr!" stated Malcolm emphatically. "The bunnet's bad anough, but yer runkly green boots makes ye look as if ye'd pinched the hin' legs affa croacadile."

Melanie sighed. "Man, your merr squerrer than a perra dice," she said. "Ye're jist a cube from Squerrsville, daddy-o."

So saying she produced a cigarette holder and inserted a cigarette in it. The holder was a metal telescopic affair, and Melanie extended it until it was somewhere in the region of two feet long.

"In the name o' hivvin!" exclaimed Malcolm. "Whit's this ye've goat noo?"

"You wouldny gerrit, man," the mod-bird told him, puffing serenely. "This is strictly for the mods. It's gear, man, real kinky!"

"Only somebody wi' a kink wid use a thing like that," said Malcolm.

Melanie turned quickly to make a fiery retort. It was more fiery than she planned. The lighted cigarette at the end of the holder seared across Malcolm's nose in a shower of sparks.

"Ya stupit dope ye!" he yelled. In a temper, he snatched the cigarette holder from her and bent it double.

It was then the young lady removed her cap. "Ah'll belt the ugly big dial aff ye, ya rotten scunner!" she yelled, proceeding to belabour her cavalier over the countenance with her headgear.

In court next day on charges of breach of the peace, Malcolm and the mod-bird glared with hate at one another when the magistrate fined them each £2.

■ **Ya stupit dope ye**. You stupid idiot. An unfortunate description even in the bland tones of southern Anglish. There is a hint of tautology — "stupid" and "dope" serve the same function. But with the accent nuances available to a native Glaswegian there is a vehement intonation that can be framed around "stupit" that makes this a greatly disparaging term.

■ **Stuck oan yer napper.** Placed upon your head. Again, an expert exponent of the Glaswegian can weave stresses and rhythym into the phrase that will encompass observation, sarcasm, humour and criticism all at the same time. It is a spoken sound that contains a facial expression, even if you can't see the person doing the talking.

■ **Runkly.** Wrinkly.

Two jealous dames put Jim in a jam

THERE was no doubt about it, Anna was an extremely pretty young lady.

Unfortunately, she was only too well aware of her beauty. This caused her to be confident, but also somewhat aggressive, not to mention boastful.

"Ah jist canny help it if fellas get a crush oan me," she confided to a group of young lady friends in the café.

"Aye. It must be a hangava nuisance bein' run efter by a' thae fellas," commented Wee Carol with more than a hint of dryness in her tones.

"Well, that's wan thing YOU'LL never be boather't wi'," retorted Anna.

"Naw, and Ah widny want tae be," Wee Carol assured her. "Ah'm quite content wi' wan man."

"Aye, Carol's goat a smashin' financy," said the small girl's particular friend, Chrissie.

"That's merr than the rest o' us kin say."

"Ach, Ah coulda been engaged twinty times over!" bragged Anna. And, turning to Wee Carol, she said, "Yer financy, Jim, wiz very interestit in me nutt so long ago, ye know."

Wee Carol received this revelation with perfect calm. "Oh, he's STILL very interestit in you," she said. "Ye see, he's been studyin' psycho-ology an' 'nat."

"Oh aye. An' whit's that goat tae dae wi' ME?" asked the glamour girl.

"Well, he says you're a type," disclosed Wee Carole. "No' bad lookin', but empty-heidit an' ett up wi' coanceit."

"Aw, he's jist sayin' that because Ah gi'ed him the brush-aff at the dancin'!" cried Anna triumphantly.

"Oh aye, he tell't me aboot that," said Wee Carole. "But he wiz jist annoyed, no' he'rtbroken.

"He dizny like rudeness, ye see. Ye don't jist say 'Naw!' when a fella asks ye tae dance."

At that very moment, Jim entered the café.

"Here's yer precious financy noo!" said Anna.

Jim joined the young ladies at the table. "Well, ur we gaun' tae the dancin', hen?" he asked Wee Carol.

"Aye, but you huv a cuppa coaffy first," said she.

He ordered a cup, and as he sat sipping it, he became aware of the fact that Anna the Siren was directing a languishing look at him, together with a seductive little half-smile she felt was alluringly effective.

"Whit's up wi' YOU?" asked Jim.

"Whiddye mean?" countered the glamour girl.

Adopting a studious pose, the young gent countered, "Ye're sittin' therr wi' yer mooth twistit up as if ye hud indigestyon or somethin'."

"Naw, naw!" exclaimed Wee Carol. "Ye dinna unnerstaun. That's hur gi'en ye wan o' hur irry-resistible smiles. You're supposed tae be a' over inflatulatit right away when ye get that smile!"

"Aw, Ah'm no' tryin' tae get aff wi' yer lumber!" snapped Anna. "Ony fella that's stupid anough tae get engaged tae a wee toerag like you dizny appeal tae ME!"

For two seconds Jim brooded over this double-edged insult.

Then – "Big-heidit nitwit!" he said, giving the beauteous Anna a cuff on the side of the head.

Screeches filled the air.

Anna gave Jim a bang on the broo with a sugar bowl, and the table went over with a crash before the police were called in to end the melee.

In court, Anna directed a look of detestation at Jim and he promptly reciprocated.

They each pleaded guilty to breach of the peace charges, and were still looking at one another with hate when they paid their £4 fines.

■ **Ett up wi' coanceit.** Eaten up with conceit. A deadly insult.

■ **Lumber.** Partner. The term can mean a male or a female. While it retains a modicum of comedic meaning (the derivation is a person you are lumbered with) it has passed into such common usage as to be a non-insulting term for a boy or girl friend.

■ **Toerag.** Highly derogatory term meaning cheap, common and annoying all in one word. The etymology points to mediaeval times when poor people wore rags bound around their feet because they couldn't afford shoes. The rags themselves wouldn't have been pleasant items after a period of use.

Skinny boyfriend gets Rosie a' embarrassed

IT was a gay party that set off for a sunny day out at the seaside in two cars.

Gayest of all was Rosie. For she was with Don, her new boyfriend, on whom, to use a technical phrase, she was "ferr stuck."

Soon after arriving at a reasonably quiet beach, the young gents and their fair companions changed into bathing attire and headed for the water.

"Wherr Don?" cried Rosie joyously as she cavorted amidst the waves.

"Here um!" came an answering voice, as Don popped his head above the surface.

"Oh, fur hivvin's sake!" gasped the young lady in amazement.

It was small wonder she was amazed. Her boy friend's long hair was plastered close to his face, and she observed for the first time that he had rather a pointed cranium.

Not only that. He was much thinner than she had imagined. A few minutes later, when he ran up on the sand, he displayed a pair of matchstick-like legs.

The all-seeing eyes of Wee Elaine caught the look of disillusionment on Rosie's face as she gazed in fascinated horror at her boy friend's lack of physique.

"Tarzan better watch hissel' or a crab might come oot fae under a stane an' rin away wi' him," said the small girl maliciously.

"Yer pal should take wan o' thae fizzicul cultur' courses an' build hissel' a new boady," said another damsel. "Urrawise he's gonny slip doon a stank wan o' thae days,"

"Aw, shut yer faces," requested Rosie, though her admiration for Don had turned to embarrassment.

When he ran up to her and suggested they should go in for another dip, he was met by a sulky shake of the head.

"Sup wi' ye?" cried the thin young gent. "Ye canny lie aboot therr a' day! Ye'll pit oan weight if ye don't take ony exercise!"

Rosie looked up at him bleakly. "Ah think you've been takin' too much exercise," she told him.

"Whiddye mean?" asked Don, bewildered. Wee Elaine was

kind enough to explain. "She didny think ye wiz sae skinny!" she said laughingly.

"Oh, so ye've been discussin' me," said the young gent angrily.

"Ah never sayed a word aboot ye," said Rosie. "Ah've jist been lyin' here lookin'."

"Aw, admit it, hen!" cried Wee Elaine, the mischief-maker. "Yer mooth fell open wi' shock when ye realised ye wiz gaun' aboot wi' a scerrcraw."

"Haw, you can beat it or Ah'll gi'e ye wan oan the gub!" Don exclaimed angrily.

The small girl retired quickly from the scene.

On the way home, Rosie had lost much of her sparkle. Don was not long in noticing this fact.

When they got out of the car, he said, "Thur no' much fun takin' YOU oot if ye're gonny be as dull as ditchwatter."

"Aye? Then don't boather takin' me oot again!" cried Rosie promptly.

"That's okay wi' me!" declared Don. "Ah'll find somebody wi' merr life aboot them!"

"Aye, an' Ah'll find somebody wi' merr flesh aboot them!" retorted the young lady. "Ah don't want tae be lumber't by nae walkin' skelington."

Don's attenuated frame shook with rage, and he gave Rosie a slap on the face.

She reciprocated by giving him a thump on the skull.

The violent, and noisy, end to their romance was observed by members of the Glasgow police force, and they were booked for disturbing the peace.

"Ah shoulda got ma eyes testit afore Ah went oot wi' THAT skinny scunner," said Rosie, as the magistrate fined them each £2.

■ **Slip doon a stank**. Slide down a street drain. Drain is such a pedestrian, un-illustrative Anglish word — while stank says so much more. You can smell the word "stank" as well as read it.

■ **Gaun' aboot wi' a scerrcraw**. Going about with a scarecrow. The "gaun' aboot wi" phrase signifies winchin', a lumber, a proto-romantic situation.

A pink shirt lands Bobby in a pickle

IT was Friday, and Bobby couldn't get home quickly enough from his work.

That night he was due to have his first date with Eileen, a prepossessing damsel he had eyed admiringly at the dancing for a long time, three weeks at least.

He was determined to make the very best of efforts with his appearance.

On would go the best suit and the high-collared white shirt he wore on special occasions.

But things did not go at all well with him when he got home. First of all, in his haste to finish his evening repast, he put a large and too-hot piece of pie in his mouth.

"Waah. Ma mooth's burnin'!" he cried, jumping up.

There was a sharp crack as he hit his skull on the kitchen pulley, which his sister, Margaret, had lowered to remove a pair of stockings.

"It's yer ain fau't," his mother, Big Meg, told him. "Ye're guzzlin' awa' therr like a stervin' dug in a black pudden facturry. Whit's yer bloomin' hurry?"

"Ah've goat a date!" Bobby informed her indignantly. "Ah've goat tae get waashed an' dressed yit!"

He finished his meal, after blowing on it, and rushed off to wash his Beatle-style locks.

Soon he was back in the kitchen, a towel wrapped round his soaking tresses.

"Wherra herr-dryer?" he asked.

"It's burstit," Margaret told him.

"Aw, inna name o' the wee man!" wailed the young gent.

"Howumma gonny gerrit dry in time? It never lies the same when Ah don't pit a net oan it an' dae it wi' the dryer!"

He rubbed frantically at his locks with the towel.

Then came the delicate business of combing his tresses into position.

"Ah tell't ye it's no' hingin' right!" he complained loudly.

"Oh, Ah think it's luvly," observed his sister, with more than a hint of mischief. "It makes ye look like a cross between Twinkle an' Dr Who."

A few seconds later a loud cry of dismay came from the bedroom, and Bobby reappeared in the kitchen.

"Whit – whit the divvle's THIS!" he yelled, holding out a bright pink shirt.

"It's yer white shirt," said Margaret. "Ah never thought the rid wid run oot the pilla slips like that."

"It wiz jist a wee accident."

"A wee accident?" cried the young gent in anguished tones. "Naw, it's a dampt disaster!"

"Ah think it's a nice colour, that pink," said Margaret. "It'll go well wi' yer guid green suit."

Bobby was almost speechless with rage, but did manage to summon some words to chastise his sibling. "Ya wee bizzim, Ah'll parrylyse ye!" he roared, raising his fist.

But the blow never landed.

Big Meg intervened, giving him a thump on the face that sent him staggering back.

The ensuing rumpus culminated in Bobby being booked for a breach of the peace.

He was very contrite when he appeared in court next day and glumly paid a £2 fine, but did have a complaint to make. "Ah nivvir did get to go oan the date, is aw," he said.

■ **A stervin' dug in a black pudden facturry**. The imaginative metaphor is a staple part of the language of Glasgow. The more admired native-speakers can summon a florid and cuttingly-apt comparison with ease.

■ **Howumma gonny gerrit?** How am I going to get it? An example of the streamlined qualities of the language. The Glaswegian and Anglish versions mean the same, but the Glasgow version contains three words, while the Anglish equivalent has six words. Native Glaswegian speakers use the time saved by this syllable economy wisely, to inject feeling, emphasis and meaning into the pared-down words. Linguists studying this morphophonology have highlighted the economy-stress-enunciation parabola, with many concluding that terms such as "gerrightintythum" conveys many more nuances of meaning than the standard Anglish equivalent. It is another illustration proving the offshoot Anglish hasn't quite captured the full flavour of the original language.

■ **Burstit**. Malfunctioning.

Brenda draws the teeth o' a man-eatin' blonde

B RENDA, her face alight with joy, faced her guests at the party she was giving.

"Big Phil's been oan the tillyphone!" she cried. "He's poppin' in tae see us!"

Screeches of delight came from the young lady guests. For this was, indeed, momentous news.

They were actually going to see at close quarters a celebrity, Big Phil, who had his own pop group and had played some gigs at the local social club (this may or may not have been the Okeydokey Club).

"Oh, that's marvellous!" shrilled Wee Karin, the pocket-sized blonde bombshell. "Ah've aye fancied Big Phil, ever since he begun his career six munse ago. Ah KNOWED then that he'd become a star!"

Brenda counselled calmness. "Now, we don't want tae crood roon' him," she said. "He'd like it merr better if we treatit him as if he wiz jist an oardinary fella."

So, when Big Phil, a picturesque figure in his purple shirt and skin-tight shiny jeans arrived, he was not mobbed.

Wee Karin gazed upon him, fascinated.

But then, greatly to the annoyance of her hostess and her fellow guests, she plumped herself down on the divan beside her hero. "Ah'm wan o' yer biggest fans!" the small blonde told him breathlessly.

"Ah think ye're ra tops, so Ah dae!"

"DAE ye?" said the star. "It's nice tae huv a fan that's as good lookin' as you."

After this exchange of compliments they chatted for quite some time, oblivious of the angry glares directed at the pocket blonde.

Brenda did her best to end their conversation. "Haw, Phil, d'ye want anurra drink?" she asked her celebrated guest.

"Naw, Ah'll no' boather," said he without taking his eyes off Wee Karin's face.

Eventually Big Phil rose to his feet. "Ah'll huv tae go," he informed Brenda. "Thanks fur the drink."

"Ah'm gaun' tae," said Wee Karin.

"Ah'm gaun' doon tae Danny's Dunny (a local dancing establishment) wi' Big Phil!"

For close on three seconds Brenda was speechless. Then, "Ya rotten wee midden!" she cried. "Ye don't give naebuddy a chanst tae talk tae ma guest, then ye calmly get up an' say ye're leavin' the pairty!"

And to underline her disapproval she gave the small blonde a thump on the skull that demolished her high bouffant hairdo.

Big Phil, star, mindful of his image, fled the scene.

But the fracas he left behind, although on the third floor of the tenement, became so noisy that the police had to be called.

The principal contestants, Brenda and Wee Karin, were booked for breach of the peace.

"She spile't ma date!" complained the small blonde in court.

"Ah'll spile yer dial if Ah ever see it in ma hoose again!" declared Brenda.

Order had to be restored in court before the magistrate could tick them off and fine them £3 each.

■ **Crood roon' him.** Crowd round him. The Glasgow term manages to convey both the act of crowding, and disdain for those who might do such a thing.

■ **Ye don't give naebuddy a chanst.** You didn't give anyone else a chance. A seeming peculiar mixture of grammatical tenses, but the intention is not only to describe Wee Karin's actions, but also to point out that she is the type of person who would have been suspected to be likely to indulge in this type of behaviour, AND might be expected to do the same thing again in future. It is a peculiar omni-tense that was/is/will be difficult for non-native speakers to grasp.

■ **Spile yer dial.** Spoil your face. A quite frightening threat in a city once renowned as the razor capital of the UK. You never know how deep such a threat might go.

■ **Naw, Ah'll no bother.** The word "Naw" in its Glaswegian form is longer (the "aw" sound being held) than the Anglish "No". This multiplies the negative. When "Ah'll no bother" is added it becomes summarily dismissive, which would have added to Brenda's ire.

A steak pie gets Sanny in a stramash

SANNY groaned. "That's the last time Ah eat yer sister's steak pie!" he informed his wife, May. "Ah've been up the hale night wi' ma stummick!"

"It's no' Mina's steak pie that upset yer stummick," said May. "It's jist that ye've went an' ett too much o' it."

"Away ye go!" cried her husband. "Ah only hud a wee daud o' it, but it wiz anough tae gi'e me the colic."

"How is it that AH'M a' right an' AH ett some o' Mina's steak pie?" May asked him.

"Because you've goat a stummick that could digest nails," said Sanny.

"Ah've goat a delicate stummick," he went on. "An' Ah shouldny be expectit tae eat greasy hame-made steak pie."

"Trust you tae look a gift horse in the mooth!" May exclaimed.

"Aye, it wiz horse she hud in that pie," growled Sanny. "Ah shouldny've pit it in ma mooth."

He was going into a further, colourful and richly detailed account of his symptoms when Mina, the giver of the steak pie, called to visit.

"Haw, yer steak pie jist aboot done fur me!" Sanny told her, with tactless candour.

The lady Mina, a woman of considerable breadth, bent an acidulous eye toward him. "Whit ur ye talkin' aboot?" she inquired.

He explained about his upset stomach and the rainbow of experiences he had suffered in the water closet over the course of the night.

"Well, ma pie hud nuthin' tae dae wi' it!" said Mina, with tones of finality. "It wiz best steak fae Johnnie McPheerson, the butcher oan the corner.

"May, here, ett the pie, an' ma Maw hud a great big daud fur hur supper, an' neethur o' them wiz up nor doon."

"It's the way he eats," May pointed out. "He gulps doon his food like a coallie dug."

"By crivvins! That's rich. Ah tell ye, Ah'm dampt sure Ah

don't shift ma chuck as quick as you tubby perr an' yer auld fat maw shift it!" said the gent.

"Oh, so May an' me an' wur maw is a buncha gluttons?" asked Mina with asperity, leaving aside for the moment the references to her family's collective girth.

"Well, let me tell you – that's the last bitty o' steak pie you'll get fae me. Ah that good beef coast me a fortune, an' you're STILL moanin'."

"That doesnae boather me," Sanny told her. "Ah widny pit anurra bit o' yer steak pie in my mooth if ye gave me a fiver! Youse yins might be able tae eat cheap meat, but no' me!"

"Oh, ya ungrateful ned ye!" cried May. "Efter Mina comin' a' the way fae Drumchapel wi' that pie!"

And with this observation she smote her husband across the face with the flat of her hand.

A noisy scrimmage followed, during which Mina fled from the house uttering that well-known Glasgow cry – "Murder Polis!"

The police soon established that only May had committed an assault, and she appeared next day in court.

"It wizny me that gi'ed him that black eye," she told the magistrate. "He catched his face oan the edge o' the table when he fell aff his cherr."

She was indignant when the magistrate, not believing this story, fined her £4.

■ **Wee daud/great big daud**. Daud is an indeterminate amount, but there are limits on the size of a daud. A serving of food that qualifies as a "daud" could probably be delivered with one hand, although, confusingly, several spoon or even ladle-fuls could still amount to one daud. Current legislation (the Weights and Measures Act 1985) is strangely silent on the dimensions of a daud.

■ **Youse yins.** You ones, you people.

■ **Shift ma chuck.** Eat my food. There is little finesse or polite manners implied in the phrase "shift ma chuck". Respectable ladies, such as the Queen, the Princess Royal, or thon wummin fae Hyndland, would not "shift their chuck".

■ **Coallie dug**. Collie dog. Famous (it would appear) for their abilities to eat quickly.

Ding-dong over bowlly Betty, the belle o' the multi-storeys

DAVIE and his generously-upholstered wife, Betty, were delighted with the balcony of their new abode in the multi-storey flats.

They put out two deck chairs and prepared to sunbathe.

"Oh, this is rerr!" Betty called to her husband, as she lay out on the balcony in her white bikini, proudly showing off her, as she thought, voluptuous figure.

"Hurry up an' get oan yer bathin' trunks. It's like the Rivvyeeria out here!"

At that moment came a discordant sound – the coarse cackle of ribald laughter. From a nearby balcony, Myrna and her visitor, Sadie, had espied the sunbather.

"Oh, did ever ye see the like o' that!" cried Myrna. "Fur a saicint Ah thought it wiz a Polar berr that hud strayed oan tae the balcony!"

"By George, Ah widny werr a bikini if Ah wiz as bowlly as HUR!" commented Sadie.

Betty twisted round in her chair. "You shut yer faces or Ah'll phone fur the polis!" she shouted angrily.

The threat had the desired effect of reducing the ladies to silence. But they were still watching.

When Davie appeared in his swimming trunks their laughter started up afresh, with an even more raucous tone than before.

"Oh, the puir sowl!" cried Myrna. "Thur haurdly an unce o' flesh oan him. Oh, that's a sin! She must snaffle a' the grub an' gi'e him hee-haw!"

"It's a peety she couldny gi'e him a transfusion o' flesh," said Sadie. "She could easy sperr him two or three stane."

"Oh, he's tryin' tae pit up his deck-cherr noo," Myrna pointed out with more laughter, "He's getting' a' mixed up wi' it. He canny tell the difference between his wee matchstick legs an' the widden legs o' the cherr."

As Davie continued to struggle with the recalcitrant deck chair, he brought forth further tempests of laughter from the keenly interested ladies.

Betty rose in her wrath. "Ah'm no' gonny warn youse again!"

she roared. "Wan merr remark oota ye an' Ah'm gonny phone the polis an' complain!"

Myrna and Sadie decided that discretion was the better part of valour, and they retired into the house.

That evening, Myrna was standing at the bus stop en route to the bingo when Betty approached her.

Myrna didn't recognise the bikini-wearer with her clothes on.

"Ur you the wumman that huz the raggedy bed-mat hingin' ower the railin' o' hur balcony?" queried Betty.

"Whit ur ye talkin' aboot?" asked the unsuspecting lady in indignant amazement. "Whit's ma bed-mat goat tae dae wi' YOU?"

"Oh, so ye UR the ignorint hauf-wit that wiz passin' remarks aboot me an' ma man!" Betty cried, and she gave Myrna what was later described by a witness as "a quick belt oan the gub".

Then she hurried back to her skyscraper home.

Later, Betty was interviewed by the police, and frankly admitted that she had taken the law into her own hands under provocation.

In court, she gave the magistrate a full account of how she had been deeply "humiliatit". He showed a measure of sympathy, and, after warning her to keep her hands to herself in future, told her to go.

■ **Bowlly.** Bow-legged. Myrna and Sadie must have seen Betty walking on to the balcony, as it would have been difficult to judge her bow-leggedness if she was relaxing on a deck-chair. However, this account of events doesn't give detail on whether the two laughing ladies were higher up than Betty, where her bowlly qualities may have been instantly apparent. Thankfully, no photos exist to verify this.

■ **Haurdly an unce.** Hardly an ounce. Yet again, an example of the withering tone that the guid Scots tongue can add to a simple phrase.

■ **Belt oan the gub.** Punch on the face.

■ **Gonny phone the polis.** Going to call the police. Compare the reaction to this threat in those days, to what might be expected nowadays. A promise to contact the local constabulary to tell of a (fairly mild) verbal insult was enough to temporarily cow the insult-givers' into silence. Would that happen in the 21st Century? Respect for authority figures in society has changed.

An unlooked-for salesman has Big Bill bilin'

THE attractive sisters, Karin and Charlotte, smiled sweetly upon the cronies, Big Bill and Wee Frank, when they met at the dancing.

"Would youse two like to come to our party on Tuesday?" Karin asked them.

"Oh, we'll be delightit!" cried Wee Frank. "It's very nice of ye askin' us."

"Very nice, so it is," put in Big Bill warmly.

Later that evening, the cronies discussed the invitation.

"Heh, that's rerr!" enthused Big Bill. "Two luvly birds invites us tae a pairty an' they never mentioned bringin' bottles nor nuthin'."

"Aw, well, Karin an' Charlotte's goat class," said Wee Frank. "Ah could tell that when we wiz huvvin' a coaffy wi' them. They aye sayed 'please'."

"Ah noticed that," said Big Bill. "It wiz – 'See us ower the sugar, please,' an' "shove us alang the choaclit biscuits, please.' It'll be a pleasure gaun' tae thur pairty."

And so the great day arrived.

At first, when they arrived at the sisters' home, it seemed as if their optimistic prognostication would be fulfilled. Like their hostesses, all the young lady guests looked most prepossessing.

"Jings!" exclaimed Wee Frank ecstatically under his breath. "Will ye take a look at the talent! Every wan o' them's an absaloot honey!"

"Let's sit in this coarnur fur a wee while an' look," breathed Big Bill in reverent tones.

They sat down on a small sofa to survey the pulchritudinous array.

Soon they were joined by an elderly gent they'd heard addressed as Auld Erchie. It turned out he was the father of Karin and Charlotte.

"Have youse two ever thought o' the future?" Auld Erchie asked Wee Frank.

"Naw," muttered the small chap, his attention taken up by a seductive and sinuous brunette.

"Ye want tae prepare for the future, though," said the elderly gent. "Noo, lissen tae me, Ah've got some very good advice tae gi'e ye baith."

He tugged at the cronies' arms so that they were forced to face him. "Ah'm talkin' about insurance!" declared Auld Erchie. "Ah kin arrange endowment policies for you two fellas."

"Aw, don't bother," said Wee Frank. "Ah want tae talk tae that young lady over therr."

"Plenty o' time for that," said the insurance expert. "Ah want tae explain how youse can get a thousan' poun'."

"Ye'll huv tae excuse us," said Big Bill.

"Don't be so impatient!" exclaimed the father of their hostesses, laying a restraining hand on each. He proceeded to give them a long sales talk. There seemed to be no escape.

"Look, we're at a pairty!" protested Wee Frank. "We don't want tae talk business."

"This is mair importanter than the pairty," Auld Erchie thundered.

It was then that Big Bill's patience ran out. He grabbed someone's tumbler from a nearby small table and dashed the contents in the elderly gent's face.

"Oh, he flung limmanade ower ma farra!" cried Karin.

"Dampt hooligan!" cried Auld Erchie.

"Pit the perra them oot!" counselled the small gent who'd been dancing with Charlotte.

For this advice, and possibly because he was nearest, he received a quietening thump on the face from Big Bill.

Amidst a medley of shouts and screeches, the cronies were ejected into the custody of the police.

"A' that talent an' we hud tae get mixed up wi' a stupit aul' chancer!" Big Bill said disgustedly next day in court as he stumped up his £3 fine.

■ **Flung limmanade ower ma farra.** Threw lemonade over my father. The world is a different place today. This story, at root, describes a physical attack on a man whose only "crime" was to attempt to inform two other men of their life insurance options. There followed a more serious attack on a man who complained that an elderly gentleman had limmanade dashed in his face. Today, even though no one was seriously hurt, a far more critical light would be shone upon these events. There would be no question of humour being attached to this.

■ **Absaloot honey.** Highly attractive young lady.

Remarks about her face mak' Phyllis fighting mad

WEE Daisy and her friends out doing their morning shopping could scarcely believe their eyes as they gathered at the local shops.

Big Phyllis had appeared amongst them wearing quite a plaster of make-up.

It was bright-green eye shadow, black-lined eyes wth jet black lashes and vivid, shiny lipstick.

"Oh, inna name o' hivvins!" cried Wee Daisy. "Whit oan earth huv ye did tae yer face?"

"Whiddye think?" rasped Big Phyllis. "Ah've jist hud a treatment."

"Whit wiz ye treatit fur – soaft'nin' o' the heid?" queried the small lady.

"Shut yer face or Ah'll knoack it up amongst yer herr!" Big Phyllis thundered.

Then to the assembled ladies she explained, "Ma niece huz goat a joab at wan o' thae beauty coonters, an' she's gi'ed me the cosmetic treatment."

"It certainly makes ye look different," commented one of the ladies cautiously.

"Aye, it dizny hauf!" Wee Daisy cried. "It looks as if a miracle hud happen't and hur wee man hud gave her two black eyes."

"That's whit YOU'LL get if ye don't cley up, ya tatty-lukkin' wee dwarf ye!" retorted the large lady. "Ye'd think she'd never saw onybody wi' make-up oan afore."

"Did yer niece pit it oan fur ye?" came another query.

"Oh, aye," said Big Phyllis, "she took nearly hauf-an-oor tae pit this oan afore she went tae her work this moarnin'.

"She's goat a flair fur a' the new styles o' make-up, ye know."

There was general agreement that the niece indeed had access to new make-up colours, and possessed innovative and unusual ideas on how it might be applied.

This led to some further questioning.

"Here Phyllis, ye'll shairly no' go tae yer bed wi' a' that stuff oan?" said yet another of the ladies.

"Of course nutt!" said the made-up one. "All this'll come aff afore ah go tae ma bed the night. But ma niece'll come up an' pit a mud pack oan ma face an' Ah'll take IT aff in the moarnin'."

"Dae us a' a favour," said Wee Daisy. "Keep it oan!"

"Wid ye lissen tae who's critycisin' me fur werrin' a wee bit make-up!" exclaimed Big Phyllis. "She went inty the chemist's an' asked fur somethin' fur her wrinkles an' the chemist gi'ed hur a tube o' liquid cement."

"Ah've a better complexion than YOU huv, by a long chalk!" protested Wee Daisy. "An' ye're two-faced onyway – an' they're baith ugly."

"It's time ye gi'ed yer mouth a rest," warned Big Phyllis. "Afore Ah pit yer face oota shape."

"It's YOUR ugly big dial that's a' oota shape!" cried the small lady. "It's no' funny-coloured make-up you need – it's a poke ower yer heid."

Choice words continued to be exchanged and soon a physical tussle, not unlike a rugby scrum but much noisier, was in progress outside the sweetie shop.

It was stopped by the police, and in court next day the warring ladies had to stump up £2 each.

"A' becuzz o' her daft-lukkin big green face," muttered Wee Daisy as she paid over her fine.

■ **Whit oan earth huv ye did tae yer face?** New styles of make-up arrived with new fashions, new types of music and new attitudes. There was a stark choice for young ladies — whether to adopt the daring new looks early, or wait until they were more widespread.

■ **Soaft'nin' o' the heid**. Softening of the head. Being soft in the head (not right in the head) was a common accusation.

■ **Cley up, ya tatty-lukkin' wee dwarf ye**. To "cley up" is to fall silent. Tatty-lukkin' (tattered-looking) is quite an insult among women who pride themselves on their appearance.

■ **A poke ower yer heid.** A paper bag over the head to keep from frightening others with ugliness. Poke, for bag, probably comes from the French poque, meaning a small sack. The word "pocket" has the same root. It is unusual to discover anything useful coming from outwith Scotland. A poke ower yer heid is a damning assessment of looks.

Jim gi'es a two-timer the aul' wan-two

JIM was overjoyed when Denise, a striking blonde he'd been chatting to at the dancing, agreed to accompany him on a trip to the coast for the day.

It had taken him a lot of time, over the course of several weeks, to persuade her.

However, she attached some conditions to the date. "Ah'll huv tae be back hame at hauf-past sivvin at night," she told him.

"Ah don't like tae be too long away fae ma Maw. She's no' keepin' too weel."

The young gent readily agreed to this. "Aw aye. Ah'll huv ye back in plenty time," he said, gazing fondly upon the beauteous blonde.

The sun shone steadily as the train headed for Largs. But Denise found cause for discontent. "That's a hangava breeze," she said. "Shut that windae afore ma herr gets blew tae bits."

"Okay," said Jim. And the window stayed closed until the train arrived in Largs.

"Oh, um Ah gled tae get affa rat train!" cried Denise as she stumbled down the platform. "Ah thought Ah wiz gonny suffycate."

"Ah, well, we'll get a braith o' the briny when we get oan tae the prom," Jim promised.

But still the weather conditions did not meet with the blonde's approval.

"That dampt wind is still therr!" she complained. "Ma herr'll be an awfy sight afore we get back tae Glesca."

And she went on in the same vein all afternoon.

Jim was not sorry when the time came for them to get back to the city.

"Ah'll see ye hame," he said at the station.

"Naw, ye don't hiv tae boather," said Denise. "Ah'll manidge fine masel'."

"Aw, Ah'll take ye hame," said Jim.

"Ah sayed naw, ye don't need tae boather!" Denise again told him firmly.

But he insisted it wasn't far, and walked her to the entrance to her close.

"Well, cheery-bye," said the blonde hastily when they got there. "See ye aroun'."

"Whissa hurry?" Jim asked her.

"Look, it's ma murra, like I sayed. Ah've goat tae get up an' see hoo –" Denise began. Her explanation was cut short by the arrival of a car.

As soon as it stopped, the young gent at the wheel popped out his head and cried, "Haw, Denise, Ah've jist made it!"

"Aw, so THIS is why ye waantit tae get back fur hauf past sivvin!" exclaimed Jim. "Ye've goat tae keep yer timetable o' dates, eh?"

At this moment, the young gent from the car strolled up. "Is the chump annoyin' ye?" he asked the blonde.

"He's annoyed me the hale bloomin' day!" declared Denise.

"Aw, we'll soon pit an end tae THAT!" said the newcomer.

But before he could implement this promise, he received a clout from Jim that sent him reeling backwards across the pavement.

With some slight exaggeration, Denise screeched out "Murder!" before Jim silenced her with two quick slaps.

The police arrived speedily and Jim was motored to the police office and charged with assault.

"Wisht Ah'd never clapped eyes oan that blastit bad-temper't blonde!" he growled in court as he parted with £4.

■ **Braith o' the briny**. A breath of sea air. Often promised to be very good for the health. In Scotland, rarely promised to be warm.

■ **Hale**. Whole.

■ **Manidge**. Manage.

■ **Affa rat.** Off of that. Anglish words are often very like Scots words, with just a few changes in spelling and different stresses having changed the southern versions into their less expressive form. It is sometimes difficult to understand why these Anglish words haven't kept the original Scots sounds. It is perhaps that the Anglish don't know how to express themselves properly, or, more likely, to accommodate the limitations of their strange pronunciations. Many of them struggle to pronounce even the simplest of words.

Floo'ers misunderstanding results in artillery exchange

SAMMY glared across the fence at the magnificent show of peony roses in the garden of his neighbour, Fred.

"They're lovely, aren't they?" said his wife, Lottie, from the back door. "It's a peety we didnae huv nane o' thae floo'ers."

"Ach, we've got violas an' sweet peas an' amnesia an' a' that!" pointed out Sammy indignantly.

"Ah widda liked two or three o' thae pianna roses like Fred's," said his wife. "We've nae floo'ers at a' in wur gairden."

"Aw, gi'e them a chanst!" cried Sammy. "Ma floo'ers'll be bloomin' away when his paeony roses is wither't. Onybody kin stick in a few plants an' wait fur them tae grou. Ah've riz a' MA plants frae seed."

"Whaur UR yer plants?" asked Fred, as he stood in the doorway of his abode. "Ye've been diggin' an' delvin' away in that gairden o' yours fur weeks, an' a' ye've goat is a few seeck-lookin' wee things that look like weeds."

Sammy, deeply offended, replied with his own brand of ready repartee, "Ah – belt up!" he said, and he stalked into the house.

During the night a typical West of Scotland summer storm raged.

When Sammy stepped into his garden next morning he saw with malicious joy that Fred's peonies had been blown askance by the high wind.

He was surveying the scene of desolation when he was hailed by Fred. "Whit the divvle ur ye staunnin' therr smirkin' fur?" shouted the peony-grower.

"Yer floo'ers izny much tae swank aboot NOO," observed Sammy.

"Away an' raffle yersel'!" shouted the enraged Fred, bending over his fallen blooms.

Hearing her husband's voice raised in anger, Fred's larger half, Big Nettie, made her appearance.

She emitted a loud wail of dismay when she beheld the havoc amongst the peonies.

However, she was immediately under the misapprehension that Sammy was responsible. "O, ya dampt vandal!" she roared.

"Oh, the rotten spite! Bashin' doon oor luvly floo'ers. Jist because ye canny grow them yersel'!"

"Wait a minnit," said Fred, "it wizny him that done it."

Big Nettie switched her accusing glare to Lottie who had arrived on the scene. She instantly accused Sammy's wife of pulverising the peonies.

"Ye done it oota sheer badness, so ye did!" screeched the large lady.

"Ah never laid a finger oan yer ruddy floo'ers!" Lottie bellowed back. "Of course YOU widny hear the storm that blowed them doon durin' the night. Ye'd be sleepin' like a log efter the load ye took oan at the coarnur pub."

The insinuation that she had been imbibing too freely at her favourite hostelry infuriated Big Nettie.

"Ya bad-tongued midden ye!" she yelled, "Don't throw yer wicked alligations at ME!"

"Ah'll throw merr than alliagations at ye, ya stupid big stumer ye!" retorted Lottie and, stooping suddenly, she picked up a lump of turf and hurled it at Big Nettie.

The large lady attempted to duck, but the well-aimed sod of turf bounced off her cranium.

With a roar of fury she looked for a missile herself. Quite a few flew back and forth, accompanied by a barrage of screeched insults, before the police arrived and put an end to the two-way bombardment.

In court next day, on breach of the peace charges, the ladies began another furious verbal battle, each blaming the other for the cross-border artillery exchange. The magistrate called a halt to this by declaring his lack of interest in who fired the first shot and threatening to jail them both.

A concerted groan went up from both ladies when he fined them each £5.

■ **Away an' raffle yersel'.** Go away. Quickly. A widespread and commonly-used comment denoting a derisive opinion of the target of the jibe. Although being the prize in a raffle might suggest something of value, the intended meaning is the opposite.

■ **Belt up.** Shut up.

■ **Stumer.** A foolish or incompetent person.

■ **Ah've riz a' ma plants.** I've raised all my plants. Riz, a single short word for cultivated, demonstrates the efficiency and economy of Glaswegian terminology.

Betty's sly wee scheme is no rival to Z-Cars

BETTY was having some little trouble with her latest gentleman friend, Eddie.

"Ah don't know whit tae make o' him," she confided to her chum, Sadie. "He's that quiet. Never peys me a coampliment nor brings me a wee present nor squeezes ma' haun' nor nuthin'. Jist watches TV."

"By jings, he's some Cassynova that ye've goat a haud o'!" Sadie commented. "There's only wan thing ye kin do about HIM."

"Whit's that?" asked Betty eagerly. "Make him jealous," said Sadie. "Let him see he's no' the ONLY fella in yer life. Kid him oan ye've goat bagsa dates.

"Wait a minute. Ah've goat an idea! When you an' him is sittin' watchin' the TV the night Ah'll gi'e ye a ring oan the phone.

"Ah'll say Ah'm 'Phil', the boy friend that's crazy aboot ye." Betty readily agreed to the plan.

That evening, as Eddie sat beside her on the couch looking at the television screen, her eyes strayed frequently to the telephone.

When it rang she sprang up to answer it, turning the TV volume down as she reached for the phone.

"Oh, is that you, Phil?" she said to Sadie at the other end. "Oh an' ye want tae take me oot tae dinner? And then the theeaytur?"

She stole a look at Eddie. He was gazing fixedly at the silenced picture on the screen, trying still to follow the action. "Naw, Ah'm no' daen nuthin' this week," she told the imaginary Phil. "Ah jist sit an' look at the tillyvision every night."

She raised her voice for Eddie's benefit. "Oh, Ah'd LOVE tae go oot wi' ye, Phil!" she said. "Whit time oan Friday, Phil? Half-past six, Phil? Right ye are, Phil. Ah'll be there. Cheery-bye, Phil!"

"That wiz Phil," she informed Eddie when she reseated herself on the couch.

Eddie wasn't pleased. "Well he's a dampt nuisance," said her boy friend. "He's made us miss half o' Z-Cars! Ah canny staun' iggirent folk that phone ye up when ye're lookin' at TV. Do they no' know it's Z-Cars that's oan?"

"Oh, Phil's asked me oot oan Friday night," said Betty.

There was no reaction to this from Eddie. His attention was wholly on Bert Lynch and Charlie Barlow's investigations.

"Ah sayed, Phil's takin' me oot oan Friday night," the young lady said loudly, and waited hopefully for a storm of protest and an avowal of love.

Instead, Eddie nodded agreeably. "Aw, that's a' right," he said calmly. "Ma Maw's TV set'll be mendit by then. It'll be rerr lookin' at hur big 14-inch screen. That yin therr's sae wee. No' that Ah'm complainin', mind!"

"Ur ye no'?" cried Betty, jumping to her feet in a rage. "Well AH am!

"Ye've been huvvin' me oan fur a stupit mug! You're only interested in mah telly, no me!"

Her anger gave her strength, and she gave her casual cavalier such a hefty smack on the face that he slumped to the floor.

This unladylike expression of her feelings led to police inquiries, and Betty appeared in court on an assault charge.

She was philosophical when fined £4. "It's worth it tae get rid o' that glaikit big TV numbskull," she declared.

■ **Ma Maw's TV set'll be mendit**. My mother's TV will be mended. It should be remembered that not everyone owned a TV.

■ **Glaikit**. One of the more famous words in the Scottish lexicon. It is unique to Scotland and means stupid, but more than stupid. It denotes a vacant expression on the face, but more vacant than the word alone suggests. It portrays a man who not only doesn't know what is going on around him, but doesn't suspect there might be anything going on at all. Tall and clumsy men, with a less-than-perfect control of what their feet might be tripping over, or objects that their elbows might be knocking over, are particularly likely to be described as glaikit. It is the perfect insult, possibly the world's most deadly insult, and probably the insult that will be easiest got away with. The true glaikit man's answer to being described as glaikit, after doing something very glaikit, will be to glaikitly say, "Eh? Whit have Ah done noo?"

Cracks about her figure have a beauty queen fumin'

CONNIE was breathless with excitement when she told the group of young ladies in the café of her experience while on holiday in the English resort of Scarborough.

"Ah wiz runner-up in a beauty coantest!" she revealed. "Ah goat a voucher fur two poun' an' a bunch o' floo'ers an' a sash!"

"Oh, that wiz magnificent!" commented Wee Moira. "Ye'll be getting a filum test nixt. Mibbe ye'll end up as wan o' James Bond's fancy dames!"

Connie ignored the small girl's flight of sarcastic fancy.

"Of course Ah hud nae intention o' gaun' in fur the coantest," she told the company, "but the boy Ah wiz wi' sayed Ah should go in fur a laugh."

"Ah'll bet he goat a laugh a' right when he seen YOU paradin' roon'," Wee Moira said.

"It might interest you tae know that it took the judges nearly hauf an oor tae decide who should be first an' saicint," Connie informed her.

"It wiz only because the urra lassie came fae Scarabarra itsel' that she wiz pit first afore me."

"Aw, thae things happen in beauty coampatitions," sympathised one of the other young ladies. "How many wiz in fur it?"

"Twinty-three," said Connie. "Whit a cheer Ah goat when they announced Ah wiz wan o' the three finalists!"

"Ah wid like tae huv saw the twinty that DIDNY get inty the finals," said Wee Moira. "They musta been a right buncha horrors."

"Oh, there wiz wan or two horrors among them," admitted Connie. "In fac', there wiz wan wee dame therr sae ugly that she coulda passed fur your indenticat twin sister."

"You should be the last tae talk aboot onybody hain' an ugly mug," said the small girl angrily.

"Listen, Ah wiz oaffer't a joab as a model," said Connie. "Ye're no' asked tae be a model if ye're ugly, ye know."

She went on to relate how tense she was in the final stages of the beauty contest.

"The judges looked me up an' doon," she said. "Then Ah heard wan o' them say, 'She's got an Audrey Hepburn figure'."

"An' a Boris Karloff face," put in Wee Moira.

Connie ignored this snarky remark. "Ah wiz that nervous!" she went on. "Ah knowed the title wid either go tae me or the Scarabarra fluff.

"Mind ye, she wiz a heid taller than me, wi great big heels oan. An' height coonts in thae coantests, ye know."

"You'd've been a heid taller than hur," stated Wee Moira, "... if ye'd goat yer legs straighten't."

The terrible insinuation was not lost on Connie. She blenched with rage. "Ur you implicatin' that Ah've ... Ah'm ... BOWLLY?" she cried?

"Aye," said the small girl boldly. "Yer curves is in the wrang places. They're in yer legs."

"Ya shoart-leggit wee scunner ye!" shrilled the beauty winner. "Ah've stood enough o' yer dampt snash!"

She thereupon picked up a container of white sugar, a mock-crystal piece of glasswear of considerable weight, and thumped her critic on the skull with it.

Police officers were soon wading through a sea of screeching damsels, their feet crunching on spilt sugar, to apprehend Connie.

In court on a charge of assault, the beauty winner was still in an ugly temper. "Ah'm gled Ah beltit hur!" she shouted.

But she burst into tears when the magistrate reprimanded her sternly and fined her £3.

■ **Shoart-leggit wee scunner ye.** You short-legged scunner you. There is no Anglish equivalent to the word "scunner". Its meaning will pass far over the heads of those who cannot speak Scots. It takes a lifetime's immersion in north-of-the-Border culture to appreciate the term's complicated and intricate meaning. If you don't know already, you'll never know. Dinnae come crying to me, it's your own fault for not being Scottish.

■ **Oaffer't.** Offered.

■ **First an' saicint.** First and second.

■ **Scarabarra fluff.** Scarborough girl. "Fluff" means inconsequential, flighty, unintelligent. The fact the girl was from south of the border doesn't necessarily mean she was unintelligent. It is entirely possible that there might be clever women who reside in the Anglish lands.

New-style furniture gets Jean in a fankle.

G EORGE and his wife were shortly moving into a modern skyscraper flat, and were discussing the acquisition of some new and up-to-date furniture.

"Well, if we're getting' two new carpets, we canny afford tae buy nae furnitur'," said the gent. "Ye'll jist huv tae be content wi' the furnitur' we've goat fur a while."

A few minutes later, while reading a newspaper, Margaret gave vent to a cry of triumph.

"Lissen tae this!" she exclaimed. "'Modernise Your Furnitur' it says here. It's an article aboot hoo tae give yer furnitur' the 1965 look.

"Huv a gander at this. A' ye've goat tae dae is saw dauds aff the legs," pointed out Margaret. "An' ye kin dae the same wi' the cherrs an' a'."

"Sa' bits aff the legs?" queried George? "Disny sound difficult, but. Ur ye sure ye waant to dae that?"

It seemed that Margaret's mind, prompted by her newspaper advert, was made up.

So that very evening, George, under the direction of his spouse, sawed two feet off each leg of their kitchen table, and all the chairs.

Soon after, Margaret's mother, Big Jean, called. "In the name o' hivvin!" she cried. "Whit huv yiz went an' did tae yer table an' cherrs?"

Her daughter explained that they'd been modernised for the new flat. "But it's no' a doll's hoose ye're flittin' inty!" Big Jean exclaimed.

"This is the new style," George told her.

"Furnitur's a' lower noo. Take a sate an' ye'll see hoo different it feels."

Shaking her head in foreboding, the large lady lowered herself with difficulty into a sawn-off armchair, in front of the kitchen table, which had been re-labeled a "coaffee table".

"Oh, this is awfy!" she exclaimed as her knees rose to meet her chin. "Oh, help, Ah'm double't up like a deed boady in a trunk!"

Although advised to try sitting with her legs stretched out in front of her, Jean still wasn't convinced about the new furniture.

Things took a turn for the worse.

When she tried to get out of the chair, she found she couldn't.

"Haw. Get me oota this!" she cried. "Ah'm takin' the cramp noo!"

Margaret took her mother's hand and pulled, while Jean did her best to push up with her other hand.

"Mind ye don't brek the erms aff the cherr!" called George anxiously.

"It's MA erm that's gonny brek!" shouted Big Jean as Margaret pulled with all her might.

Suddenly her mother rose from the chair, but the momentum generated led her to shoot forwards, and sprawl flat on her face across the table.

There was a yell, followed by a sharp crack as one short leg of the table snapped, precipitating the large lady, with a less-than-graceful sideways roll, to land on her back on the floor.

"Ya big stupit ass ye!" roared George.

"Ye've went an' split the sate o' the cherr an' broke the leg aff wur new coaffy table!"

"Ma Maw couldny help it," said Margaret as she helped her mother to her feet.

"She's faur too fat tae be sittin' in ony cherr," said George ungallantly. "It's time she went afore she wrecks wur hoose a'thegither!"

"Ah'll wreck YOU, ya stupit-lukkin', foosty-faced nunnentity ye!" bellowed Big Jean.

She stooped, picked up the severed table leg, and bounced it smartly off her son-in-law's forehead.

In court on an assault charge, the large lady was told to control her temper in future, no matter what kind of furniture she was confronted with, and admonished.

■ **Ya stupit-lukkin', foosty-faced nunnentity ye.** You stupid-looking nonentity, with a beard. Foosty-faced could signify facial hair, but probably not the most fulsome, luxuriant of beards. It could also just mean a bad complexion. Nunnentity is possibly the 1965 fore-runner of the more modern "numpty".

■ **A'thegither.** Altogether. The Glasgow version is a more powerful, more inclusive, more complete word.

■ **Haw.** Difficult to transcribe into Anglish. The nearest would be "hey" although the intent is sometimes more aggresive. Nearer might be "Hey you, ya stumer". It is intended to grab attention, though not necessarily in a polite way.

The sad story of Carol the flirt and Wee Davie's revenge

CAROL is an extremely prepossessing damsel, with straight black hair down to her shoulders and large and expressive green eyes.

She also has the type of figure that a red-blooded chap might look twice at.

However, she is one of those tiresome young ladies who believe that every man they meet falls an instant victim to their charms.

This discomfiting discovery was made by Wee Davie a few minutes after he'd conducted her to the cocktail bar of a somewhat expensive restaurant.

"What'll ye have?" he asked as they seated themselves on stools.

"Vodka an' orange," murmured the beauteous brunette absently. Her eyes were on the handsome foreign barman.

"That big Eyetalian fella there canny keep his eyes aff me!" whispered Carol excitedly when the barman turned his back.

"Can he no'?" said the small gent grimly. "Well, feenish yer drink an' we'll go tae anurra bar where ye'll no' be sae trouble't —"

"He's awfy like Laurence Harvey!" interrupted the brunette.

"Aye," said Wee David dryly. "Laurence Harvey will be servin drinks here, of coorse he will. Well, Ah think we should get along tae the dancin' noo."

On the bus Carol discovered someone else who was apparently overcome by her beauty.

"See the look that young curly-heid't fella gave me when he goat aff the bus!" she exclaimed. "He kept sterrin' at me at the bus stoap, tae!"

"Ah never noticed," said Wee Davie glumly.

In the dance hall, the brunette declared herself to be all but surrounded by more admirers.

"They two fellas staunnin' at the door therr huv kept lookin' at me ever since we came in!" she declared. "An' half the dancefloor is lookin' ower."

Wee Davie was becoming exasperated. He decided to take

reciprocal action. "Look at that blonde doon the ha' therr," he said suddenly.

"WHIT blonde?" asked Carol truculently.

"Oh, she's went behind that buncha lassies," said Wee Davie. "She must know we're talkin aboot hur. She's been smilin' an' wavin' tae me behind your back ever since we stertit dancin'!"

Carol was highly indignant. "You musta stertit smilin' tae HUR!" she complained. "Ah don't like fellas Ah'm wi' smilin' tae urra girls!"

"Ah canny help it if a good-lookin' dame smiles tae me," said wee Davie. "Whit aboot a' the fellas ye tell me are lookin' at YOU?"

"That's diff'rint," snapped the brunette. "Ah jist happen tae attrac' men."

"Well, ye don't attrac' ME!" exploded Wee Davie. "Ah'm fed-up listenin' tae you tellin' me aboot a' the fellas that's overcame by yer fatal fascination. If you'd stoap flickerin' yer eyelashes an' daein' the coy stuff naebuddy wid boather lookin' at ye at a'."

Words failed Carol.

However, actions did not. She reached for her handbag and, with a screech of rage, brought it down on her escort's head.

For ending her romance in this abrupt fashion, the comely brunette had to disburse £2. Her coy smile was noticeably absent as she stamped angrily from the dock.

■ **Doon the ha' therr**. Down the hall there. Geographical direction often had places described as "doon". Doon the wattur", for the Clyde holiday towns, for instance. It was used much more often than "along".

■ **Urra, anurra, curly-heid't, attrac', stertit, huv.** All staple pronunciations. These words, and many like them, have different spellings, and sound different, in English. No one knows why. Perhaps there should be studies undertaken on why Anglish words aren't spelled or pronounced properly.

■ **Naebuddy wid boather**. No one would bother. It is intended as disparaging.

■ **Laurence Harvey.** An actor once described as "the perfect pin-striped screen cad". Died, aged 45, in 1973, a veteran of three marriages and various rumours about his underlying taste in partners that might have made him unlikely to have been tempted by Carol's charms.

Janet fa's oot wi' a candid friend

THE young ladies had met for lunch in a small bistro-cafe, and Janet was telling them of the wonderful evening out she had had with a new gentleman friend.

"Aw, it wiz faabyullus!" she recounted. "Norrie took me tae dinner. Of course, he choosed the food and wine an' that. He's been around, ye know."

"He's been around a' right!" commented Wee Sally. "He's auld anough tae be yer feyther!"

Janet gave her a steely stare. "How d'you know whit ma friend looks like?" she asked.

"Ah've saw him," disclosed Wee Sally.

"Me an' the boy friend wiz havin' a drink at the cocktail bar in thon hotel when you an' yer aul' friend wiz in on Saturday night."

"Ah never seen YOU," Janet said disbelievingly.

"Naw," the small girl said. "You an' Wee Tubby wiz in the dinin'-room. Ye wiz that busy feedin' yer faces that ye hudny time tae see naebuddy."

"Let me tell you – ma friend Norrie is a perfect gentleman," said Janet. "The fact that he has loads o' money means absalootly nuthin' tae me."

"Aw, stoap the kiddin'!" exclaimed the small girl. "Whit happen't when thon nice big fella ye used to be pally wi' took ye oot? Ye wiz disgustit when ye fun' oot he could only staun' ye pie an' chips an' a gless o' cream sody."

"Ah don't need tae go oot wi' cheapskates", Janet told her. "When a gentleman takes me oot fur the evenin' Ah expec' tae be treatit like a lady."

"By hivvins, Wee Tubby wiz treatin' ye a' right at that hotel!" declared Wee Sally. "Ye shiftit thon big prawn cocktail in record time. Then ye goat tore inty yer fillit steak as if ye hudny ett for munse!"

"That's a dampt lie, of course," said Janet. "Ah know how tae conduc' masel' when Ah'm dinin' oot."

"Oh, nae doot ye wiz in sparklin' form," commented Wee Sally. "But maist o' the sparks wiz comin' aff yer knife an' foark as ye walloped big dauds o' steak inty yer gub."

"Aw, gi'e yer face a rest," Janet requested. "We a' know you canny get naebuddy tae take you oot excep' that Ronnie fella. An' he's jist a heidcase".

"Aye, you think he's a heidcase because he widny gi'e ye a lift tae the dancin' in his ker wanst," stated the small girl.

"Oh, lissen tae that!" scoffed Janet. "The mug wantit me tae go for a run in his ker, but it wiz that mawkit Ah widny go inty it. Ah like tae travel in a DECENT car. Norrie's goat a Jagyur."

"Ah widny be seen wi' thon baldy-heidit wee fat fella supposin' he hud TWA Jagyurs an' a Aston-Martini threw in," said Wee Sally roundly.

"Kerz an' dinners is a' you kin think o'. Ony merr o' thae dinners an' yer gonny get even fatter than ye ur a'ready."

"Whit d'ye mean 'fatter'?" asked Janet angrily.

"A few merr o' yer fancy big dinners an' ye'll be as fat as that wee oabjic' ye're gaun' aroon' wi'," the diminutive one told her.

A moment later Wee Sally was recoiling from a sharp slap on the cheek.

The regrettable stramash concluded with Janet being booked for assault.

In court she was indignant when the magistrate fined her £2. "A coupla quid fur wan belt oan the jaw!" she exclaimed as she paid up.

"Ah shoulda knoacked hur big fat heid aff!"

■ **Wee Tubby**. Fat-shaming hadn't been identified as a bad thing.

■ **Gless o' cream sody.** Glass of cream soda. A slightly more upmarket type of pop than limminade, so Janet's former "nice big fella" friend wasn't being entirely miserly.

■ **A coupla quid fur wan belt oan the jaw!** A belt on the ja' is a punch on the face, although a "belt" sounds slightly less serious. But then casual violence — in all walks of life — was seen as less serious, hence Janet's surprise at such a small matter resulting in a fine of 40 shillings.

■ **Mawkit**. Filthy, putrid. It was originally a cheuchter term for a sheep that was infested with maggots.

■ **Jagyur. Aston Martini**. Awfy posh kerz.

Manky Minnie's shock welcome for Boozy Susie

JANE looked on with interest from the window of her home in the multi-storey flats. "Here!" she cried to her husband, Malcolm, "Somebody's took the empty flat next door!"

"Ah hope they're no' a shoo'er o' scruff," he retorted, without looking up from his newspaper.

"They're takin' the furniture oot the van noo," his wife reported. "It's a' that kinna moadern stuff. Oh, a car huz drew up, an' a man an' wumman's gettin' oot."

"A car, eh?" murmured Malcolm. "Don't tell me we're huvvin toaffs steyin' next tae us."

His words went unheard. Jane's eyes had opened wide in amazement. A sudden screech escaped her. "It's HUR!" she shrilled, recognising an auld enemy.

"It's that big wid-be that used tae be ma boss in the dress shope before we got married!"

"Ach, well, she's no' yer boss noo," said Malcolm.

"She made ma life a misery!" exclaimed Jane. "Ah'm gonny huv a word wi' hur!"

She went out to the landing just in time to meet her former boss, Netta, and her husband, Kenneth, who were just getting out of the lift.

"It's yersel'!" said Jane grimly.

"Ah'm afraid Ah don't know you," Netta said, puzzled.

"Ah recognised YOU a' right," retorted Jane. "Ye're skinnier than ever. Ah see ye've goat her wallies in. Ah mind how yer teeth used tae look like the Ten Commandments – every wan' o' them broken."

"Ah think we'd better get inty the hoose," said Kenneth hurriedly.

"Oh, Ah'm sorry," Netta said to her husband. "Ah wida intraduced ye to this lady, but Ah forget her name. Ah jist used tae cry her 'Manky Minnie'."

"That wiz nuthin' tae whit we cried YOU!" roared Jane. "The usual name wiz 'Boozy Susie.' Never aff the booze an' yer haun' never oot the till!"

"You're a witness tae thae slanders!" Netta screeched at her husband. "This is jist spite because Ah gi'ed hur the sack."

"Aye, that's whit ye were sellin' in thon so-called dress shope – sacks!" alleged Jane.

"Oh, when Ah think o' the puir mugs ye sel't that rubbidge tae at hauf-a-croon a week."

"We didny sell mony dresses the week you wiz there," said the ex-shop manageress. "The stock wiz filthy dirty wanst you got yer hauns oan it.

"Ah mind the lassie ye wiz tryin' tae sell a dress tae. You brung oot a white dress, an' she sayed she waantit a WHITE dress, no' a black-an'-white yin."

"Don't tell lies!" shouted Jane. "You couldny get rid o' me quick enough because thon big commercial traveller that came in sayed Ah wiz pretty."

"Ye didny hear him right," said Netta. "He sayed ye wiz pretty mawkit."

"You ferrly chased up thon big traveller!" Jane declared. "He wiz feart tae pit his nose in the door!"

"Naw Ah wizny!" blurted out Kenneth. There was a five-second pause before the full truth sunk into Jane's consciousness.

Then – "Don't tell me she CATCHED ye!" cried Jane.

"Wid ye credit that! Ah didny realise ye wiz as big a mug as ye look!"

Not a word came from Netta. She simply raised the small bedside table she was carrying and felled Jane with a considerable blow to the cranium.

This rough retaliation led to her appearance in court where, weeping profusely at the injustice of it all, she disbursed a £4 fine.

■ **Shoo'er o' scruff**. Respectable working-class folk would look down their noses at non-respectable members of the working class. However, it was sometimes difficult to tell where the line of demarcation lay.

■ **Yer teeth used tae look like the Ten Commandments**. Another colourful turn of phrase of the type that has always been admired among Glasgow wordsmiths.

■ **Rubbidge at hauf-a-croon a week**. Rubbish for 12.5p a week. Goods (dresses in this case) would be bought, then payed up on hire-purchase (the nivvir-nivvir).

A couple o' cheeky Mods get a meltin'

ANNE'S fancy, white, knee-high boots were obviously a copy of the expensive footwear made fashionable by the Paris dress king, Monsoor Courreges.

Wearing them with her ultra-short, kilt-like skirt, short jacket, and peaked Beatle cap made Anne feel very much that she was "with it".

She certainly caused something of a sensation when she walked into her favourite haunt, a small dance hall.

Her sartorial splendour was apparently voted "gear" by the young gentlemen present.

To her similarly Beatle-capped friend, Elsie, she said delightedly, "Thae boots huv knoacked them oot! Ah've never been liftit sae mony times since Ah stertit dancin'!"

But two pairs of disapproving eyes were watching her as she danced.

They belonged to Janice and Wee Rhoda. These young ladies considered themselves Mod girls and, to announce this important fact to the world, they wore long skirts.

"Oh, wid ye look at that sight!" Janice exclaimed. "She's like something fae outer space."

"Aye," commented Wee Rhoda. "She's the kinna thing ye'd expec' tae see in 'Dr Who.' Ah'll bet ye she's gaun' steady wi' a Dalek."

This observation caused Janice to indulge in an outburst of shrill laughter in which the diminutive damsel beside her joined.

As they laughed, they kept looking at Anne.

Anne, quite rightly, assumed that she was the subject of their mirth, and, not one to take such things lightly, over she went to them.

"Is youse perr amused at sump'n?" she asked the fair Mods.

"We're allowed tae laugh if we see sump'n funny, ur we no'?" said Janice.

"Yiz ur no' gonny laugh at ME, Ah kin tell ye that," Anne warned them. "If yiz want a REAL laugh yiz should go an' tak a dek at yersels in a mirror. Yiz look like a couple Queen Victorias in thae lang skirts."

"By hivvins, Ah'll no' say whit YOU look like in yer Courage boots," Wee Rhoda sneered.

"You widny huv the courage tae werr boots like them," asserted Anne. "Ah'm nutt surprised ye're werrin' long skirts. They're ideal fur coverin' up yer wee skinny legs."

"Oh, lissen tae who's talkin' aboot legs!" cried Janice. "Did ye get thae boots specially widened tae suit YOUR legs?"

The dread implication that she had fat legs made Anne flare up fiercely. "Ach, ye perra ault-fashint-lookin' frumps!" she yelled.

One of the white knee-boots shot up and the toe caught the seat of Janice's Mod dress.

Wee Rhoda sailed in to avenge her friend, but she received what was later termed a "scud on the skull" from Anne.

The dispute was hustled outside the hall by the ever-vigilant staff.

These events had their climax in court when Anne entered the dock on a double charge of assault.

"Aw, Ah'll plead guilty," she said airily. Her sangfroid vanished and she let out a screech of dismay when the magistrate fined her £4.

■ **Monsoor.** Monsieur Courreges. A well-known fashion designer in the 1960s. French (or any other language) when spoken in Glaswegian, should be written in a phonetic manner. Though when pronounced aloud, a slightly italicised sound (a verbal form of punctuation) should be adopted to denote the use of a dampt furrin word. However, no attempt should be made to pronounce furrin words in French (or German, Spanish, etc) accents as this would be seen as pretentious. All furrin words become Scoticised and are the better for it.

■ **Mod girls.** One of the distinctive music tribes of the 1960s. These various factions could be told apart by their mode of dress and style of dance.

■ **Voted "gear".** Judged to be sartorialy elegant and accomplished.

■ **Tak a dek**. Take a look, catch a glimpse. Thought to have originated as "tak a deek".

■ **Lifted**. Asked to dance.

Rita plays on a guitar man's nerves

THERE was a flush of triumph on the face of Wee Andy M.C., as he faced the eager throng in the Okeydokey Club.

"Ladies and gents," he said, "I beg for to intimidate to youse that I have went and made one of the most remarkable-est discoveries that have ever been made in the history of this club."

"Don't tell me ye've fun' a way o' takin' the knoats oot the flerr?" came the raucous query from Rita the Critic.

"Madam, this is not no time for none of your flippantatious remarks," said the Master of Ceremonies sternly, his beady eye falling upon an uncowed Rita.

He went on, "The announcement I am about fur to make is of some unconsiderable importance."

Turning to the assemblage he went on, "The discovery I refer to is none urrer than a highly talentated young gentleman, a singer, who goes under the nom dee plum of Caravan.

"This artiste identificates hisself with the more seriouser side of life an' that, and sings controvertical songs which he hisself has writ.

"Ladies and gents, allow me for to present ... Caravan."

The young gentleman so designated shambled into view, wearing a leather jacket and faded jeans. His long, dark hair made his sullen, pasty face seem smaller than it was. He strummed on a shabby guitar, and in a high, fluting voice sang –

"I will never join the Army,
So to youse I sing this song.
Not for me the tunes of glory,
Firing guns is all quite wrong ..."

"Heh! Heh! Cried Rita angrily. "Gi'e it a by! We don't want tae hear that rubbidge!"

The "protest singer" stopped. "You've nae right tae interrup' me!" he squeaked.

"Ya stupid-lookin' hauf-wit ye!" roared the young lady. "Whaur wid you be the noo if ma aul' man an' thoosants like him hudny jine't the sojers in the las' waar?"

Wee Andy quickly intervened in this discussion of pacifism and warmakers.

"Come, come!" he cried. "Our friend, Caravan, here, was nutt making no reference to no gents that participated in no war."

"He's makin' a fool o' sojers!" said Rita indignantly. "Fancy a peely-wally wee man like that crity99cisin' them that done thur bit in the war like MA aul man!"

"Parding me," said Wee Andy. "But I am certing that the song is not casting no aspiration on your parent or no other gents that was members of the Army."

"Ah want tae protest at the intoleration showed by this person," stated Caravan. "Ah've every right tae express ma beliefs when Ah sing ma songs."

"Ye kin sing hee-haw," Rita told him. "An' yer song's a lot o' dampt trash."

"Ma songs is meant for right-thinkin' people," the singer informed her.

"Oh, Ah think a' right," Rita shouted. "Right noo Ah think Ah'll bash your bloomin' pan in!"

Fuelled by her outrage at the perceived slight upon British military history, and several large vodkas, she rushed forward, jumped up on the band platform, and snatched the guitar from the artiste.

"Enough!" cried Wee Andy. "Kindly give the performer his instrument!"

"Aye, he's gonny gerrit," said Rita. She swung the guitar, and Wee Andy recoiled with a split second to spare as it descended on the singer's skull with a dull twung.

Almost simultaneously, the Master of Ceremonies emitted the low emergency whistle, and his henchmen materialised to escort Rita from the premises.

In court her fury was unabated. "Ah didnae hit that rotten beatnik hard enough!" she declared. The magistrate quietened her with a £3 fine.

HM Forces were not consulted on the matter.

■ **Ye've fun' a way o' takin' the knoats oot the flerr.** You have found a way of taking the knots out the floor. A good dancefloor had a little, but not too much, "slide". Floors would be sprinkled with Sliperene, a talc-like powder that might also give a shimmery effect. A dancefloor made of cheap wood, with lots of knots — especially wood that hadn't been seasoned long enough — would have sticky spots that made dancing difficult. The better dance halls would have very few knots.

■ **Ye kin sing hee-haw.** You can sing nothing/you can't sing at all. Hee-haw is a strangled oath, in the same way that "Sweet Fanny Adams" is a strangled oath. The full original meaning will not be discussed here.

A 'fab big hunk' has Nancy cuttin' up rough

BIG Nancy looked troubled when she met her friend, Joan. "'Sup wi' YOUR face?" inquired Joan.

"Ach, Ah'm fed up," confessed the large girl. "Fellas'll no' look at me because Ah'm big. Ah wisht Ah wiz YOUR size."

"Don't be daft!" her smaller friend adjured her. "Thur plenty big fellas gaun' aboot. Look at thae sojers, the Guards. Thur bags o' them."

"But they're a doon in London, 'n 'at," sighed Nancy. "Thur nane o' thum in Glesca. It's hopeless tryin' tae get a fella o' ma size here."

"Hivvins, ye're talkin' as if the shopes hud run oota them," said Joan. "Let's get alang tae the dancin'. Thur bound tae be wan or two big fellas therr."

Indeed, there were several tall young gents in the dance hall. But they all had partners.

"Wid that no' scunner ye!" said Big Nancy, scowling across the hall at a couple.

"Look at that fab big hunk owrerr. Hauf a heid taller'n me. An' who's he lumberin'? A wee dame jist hauf ma size!"

But the tall gent was unaware of Nancy's presence.

She was still staring over at him when she heard a voice at her elbow. "Ur ye furrup?" it said. Big Nancy looked round, then down.

Two feet below yer eye-level was the face of Wee Len.

Nancy was horrified at the idea of dancing with him. "Oh – err – Ah'm waitin' fur a friend," she said.

"Ye've been waitin' a hangava long time," commented Wee Len. "Ye kin dance while ye're waitin'."

At that moment Nancy saw that the small girl had left the suitably-sized gent across the floor and that he was now looking at HER.

"Er … Ah'm no dancin'," she murmured to Wee Len. Her eyes were still on the tall young gent.

"Ah kin SEE ye're no dancin'," said Wee Len. "That's why Ah'm askin' ye. It seems tae me that ye're away in a dream an' ye canny –"

He was interrupted by a cry of chagrin from Nancy. The tall

young man, obviously seeing Nancy was taken, had turned his attention to another small girl.

"Whassamarra?" inquired the small gent.

"Ya wee mug!" cried Big Nancy. "Ye've went an' spile't everythin'! 'Zat no' damnabile! He wiz comin' ower tae lift me fur a dance when you had tae butt in!"

"Whit ur ye bletherin' aboot?" asked the bewildered small gent.

"AH came over tae lift ye. Ah don't think ye've heard a word Ah've sayed tae ye!"

"Aye, Ah've heard ya craikin' awa' therr fur ages!" retorted Nancy with great asperity. "An' Ah'm no' dancin' wi ye! Ah don't dance wi' wee smouts like you."

"Ah wiz daen' ye a favour askin' ye!" said Wee Len with some spirit. "Ye'll be dampt lucky if onybody asks ye again."

In a frenzy of furious frustration, the statuesque young lady grabbed his shoulders, shook him violently and threw him to the floor.

It took two tall officials all their time to eject her and place her in the custody of two tall constables.

In court, Big Nancy looked more sullen than ever. "A fiver?" she exclaimed when fined that amount. "Efter that wee pest ruinin' ma evenin' tae!"

■ **Fellas'll no' look at me because Ah'm big.** The fashion was for women to be petite. Magazine articles would incessantly push this mantra, with never a thought for what might nowadays be termed "body-shaming". Comments such as: "And aren't her hands so small" would be passed on the likes of Princess Margaret (a major style icon of the time) and be intended as high praise.

■ **Whassamarra.** What's the matter? The word amalgamation might look odd when written, but is a perfectly normal and everyday word when uttered in a Glesca accent. It would sound strange if it wasn't one word. An added advantage is that "whassamarra" is a word that sounds the same whether the speaker is drunk or sober.

■ **Comin' ower tae lift me fur a dance.** Coming over to ask me to dance. The sequence of events was that a man would ask a woman to dance, not the other way around (unless a "ladies' choice" had been announced, which was quite rare).

■ **Smout.** Small, insignificant person. Originally a small salmon or sea trout.

Johnny's treat-em'-mean tactics land him in trouble

WEE Johnny was worried about his girl friend, Susan. "Tae tell ye the truth, Ah think she's lost her notion o' me," he confided to his friend, Arthur.

"She's aye glum when Ah'm oot wi' hur."

Arthur, something of an expert on the mysterious and complicated subject of women, declared, "Ye're no' treatin' her right."

The small gent's mouth fell open in astonishment. "No' treatin' her right!" he gasped. "Hivvins, nae dame is treatit merr righter than SHE is! If she waants to go tae the dancin' we GO tae the dancin'. If she waants a fish supper, she gets wan. If she wants –"

"Ah know, Ah know," interrupted Arthur. "That's the trouble wi' you. Burds doesny like fellas that does everythin' thae want them tae dae."

"Howrat?" inquired Wee Johnny, mystified.

"Well, ye've goat tae come the auld James Bond stuff – masterful wi' dames," explained the expert. "Ye've goat tae treat them rough. DON'T turn up on time for a date. DON'T dae whit THEY want tae dae. Be a bit difficult."

"But if Ah done a' this, Susan might no' be pleased," pointed out the unhappy suitor.

"Of course she'll no!" agreed his friend. "But she'll grow tae respec' ye. Burds likes tae be bossed aboot. They get bored wi' fellas that's subversient tae them."

Wee Johnny thought long and hard over the advice. "Ah'm gonny huv a go at the James Bond stuff," he growled.

That evening, on his way to meet the petulant Susan, he dropped into a hostelry and had two or three refreshments. These reinforced his determination to be masterful with the young lady.

"Oh, inna name o' heaven!" she exclaimed when they met. "Ye're five minnits late, an' ye've goat a smell oan ye like a distillery! Hav' you been drinkin'!"

"Naw, Ah hud nae eftershave lotion – so Ah rubbed ma dial wi' whisky," Wee Johnny told her with heavy sarcasm.

Susan blinked in surprise. "Ah don't like dancin' wi a fella wi' the smell o' drink oan him, she said.

"Who sayed we wiz gaun' tae the dancin'?" Wee Johnny asked. "As a matter of fac', Ah've decidet that we'll go ta ra flicks."

It was now apparent that the small gent's masterful Bond technique was not appreciated.

"You've WHIT?" Susan asked with dangerous calm.

"Ah've decidit we'll go tae the flicks," reiterated Wee Johnny. "Ah'm no' in the mood fur dancin' the night."

"Oh, ur ye no'?" said Susan. "Well, Ah'm sorry aboot that. But Ah'm in the mood fur dancin' an', whit's merr, Ah'm gaun' tae the dancin'!"

It was the testing moment. "We are nutt gaun tae the dancin'," Johnny declared.

"Ah know rat," retorted the young lady. "Ah'm gaun' oan ma tod, an' you kin go tae the flicks or back tae the pub, or ye kin go an' take a runnin' jump tae yersel'."

"Aw, noo, wait a minnit," began her cavalier in alarm.

"Ah waitit ten minnits fur you!" exclaimed Susan angrily. "Then ye turn't up hauf-sloashed an' gi'ed me up a lot o' buck."

"Ah wiz jist tryin' tae show ye –" said Wee Johnny.

"Aw shut yer face!" cried Susan.

She assisted him to do this by slapping him across the mouth with her handbag.

The noisy scrimmage that ensued resulted in them appearing in court on breach of the peace charges.

It was obvious the romance was over.

"The wee numbskull wiz askin' fur a belt oan the gub," stated Susan.

The magistrate fined them £3 each and they hurriedly went their separate ways.

■ **She's aye glum.** She's always displeased. Aye can mean "yes", but also "always". When meant as "always" the word will be bitten-off, a shorter syllable than when meant as "yes".

■ **Ma dial.** My face.

■ **Hauf-sloashed.** Partially drunk.

■ **Oan ma tod.** On my own. The origin of "tod" for alone, is unknown, though "tod" is an old Scots word for fox, a lone hunter.

Sammy gets the works at the works dance

THE most eligible bachelor at the works staff dance was undoubtedly the dashing Sammy, the David Niven of the drawing office.

Eagerly the group of young ladies at a corner table watched him dancing with a blonde.

"Aw he's luvly!" sighed Christine.

"Ah met him as Ah wiz comin' in," revealed Myra. "He sayed he liked ma herr!"

"Aye. He couldny miss it," commented Iris, a tinge of envy in her tones.

Myra's coiffure, heavily stiffened with lacquer, was as high as a guardsman's busby.

The young ladies followed the movements of the much-admired Sammy with breathless interest.

"He's swallied two haufs!" ran Christine's commentary.

"He's pittin' oan a funny wee polisman's hat ... oh wait a minnit, look — he's comin' ower here!"

The young ladies collectively held their breaths as he stopped and surveyed them. Then, with his easy social grace, he nodded at Myra.

"Right," he muttered.

Soon they were up and performing that graceful terpsichorean creation, the Mod.

With charming lack of conventionality, Sammy kept his cigarette in his mouth.

In the course of their convolutions, Myra whirled round. At once her partner's cigarette was whipped from his mouth to disappear, it seemed, into thin air.

In actuality, the fag had vanished into thick hair – Myra's tall hair-do.

"Heh, wherr ma fag? Wherr ma fag?" cried Sammy, searching the floor.

Myra danced on blithely for a time.

But suddenly, when the cigarette burned its way through the hirsute pagoda and reached her scalp, she gave vent to a loud screech and started beating her head.

"Ma herr's burnin'!" she yelled.

Fortunately, there was a man close by who was prepared to make a great sacrifice. He rose and poured his half-pint of beer over the burning coiffure.

The effects of fire and brewed alcoholic drink conspired to reduce her previously gravity-defying hair arrangement to a soggy, oddly-smelling wreck.

"Ye shouldny've been smokin' when ye wiz dancing," Myra raged at Sammy. "Look at ma herr. Thur a hale big daud burnt oot it!"

"Ah like tae smoke when Ah'm dancin'," the young gent explained. "An' you're the first burd that's ever complained aboot it."

Myra gave him a bleak look – then a hard kick on the shin.

As he bent to caress his leg, he received a hard chop on the back of the head from the infuriated damsel.

After they'd carried the young gent off to revive him, Myra was asked to leave.

At the door, however, the police waited to charge her with assault.

"It's no' ferr!" she protested in court. "The stupit creep jist aboot burnt the heid aff me!"

She was burning with yet further indignation when the magistrate fined her £4.

■ **Ma herr.** My hair. A beehive hair-do was no easy thing to achieve, and took no little time to mould into shape.

■ **"Right," he muttered.** The least-polite invitation to dance. Much can be assumed about Sammy's character, and his opinion of himself, from his nonchalant, indeed lazy, approach to Myra.

■ **Swallied two haufs.** Swallowed two half-measures (half a gill), probably of whisky. An admired, young-man-about-town like Sammy would be able to hold his drink.

■ **No' ferr. Herr. Wherr.** Stress should be placed on the double Rs. These are much superior pronounciations to the southern Anglish versions (fai---, hai---, whey---) which have no endpoint. The words, in Anglish, just drift off with little or no further clue to what was intended to be said in the native speakers' virtually unintelligible attempts to communicate. But in Glaswegian, these words have an easily-defined sound and a clear endpoint, and are therefore better understood.

Okeydokey floorshow has Rita raisin' the roof

T HE patrons of the Okeydokey Club were even more eager than usual as they gathered round the front of the band platform anxious to hear about the "Grand Surprise Floorshow" advertised on placards outside the noted dance resort.

Soon the impressive fanfare came from Fred and His Band of Boogie Woogie Bachles, and, with one of his most benign smiles, Wee Andy, M.C., made his entrance.

"Ladies and gentlemens," he said, "may I be permitted for to offer to youse the most heartiest best wishes for the coming New Year that has just went and dawned upon us."

"Ye'll notice he's no' oafferin' his auld customers a hauf," called Rita the Critic.

"We have more importanter things to deal with than mere alcoholical refreshments," Wee Andy pointed out, his eye on his nemesis.

"Tonight we are presenting to youse certing artistes that would do no unconsiderable credit to one of them pop shows which we see on the TV. I refer to none urrer than McGravie and the Okey-dokers!"

A long-haired young gent appeared on the dance floor with a hand microphone which trailed a long length of flex. With various anatomical convulsions he sang:-

"Ma heart's soft as a plate of curds
Whenever Ah see those pretty burds ..."

The word "burds" was the cue for "The Okey-dokers," three generously-proportioned young ladies in jeans, to enter and perform a rhythm dance. It shook the hall to its foundations.

McGravie sang on:-

"See 'em dance, like ra flowers in Spring
These sweet dolls make ma heart go zing."

With more verve than ever the young ladies stamped out the rhythm.

Then Rita recognised one of the dancers. "Oh, it's Big Betty Whiddyecryur!" she cried. "Hur that worked in the grocer's afore they fun' hur oot. Couldny keep hur haun' oot the biscuit tins."

This revelation of her past made the dancer wheel round angrily. As she did so, one of her feet caught in the flex of the hand microphone, and McGravie the singer was almost yanked off his feet. He managed to keep his balance, but the microphone was dead.

He continued to mouth the words of his song in a tinny voice, but was scarcely audible.

Meanwhile Big Betty and the two other Okey-dokers contorted their frames and stamped in time to the beat number.

When the act ended the raucous laughter of Rita rose above the somewhat half-hearted applause.

"Oh, it's a good thing it's finished. Anurra saicint an' Big Betty therr wida split the sate of her jeans!"

The Master of Ceremonies was extremely displeased. "Never have I saw such unmitiagatit conduct as you have went and perpetuatit here tonight," he told the critical young lady.

"But permit me for to intimidate to you – I am not going to put up with no furder unseenly commentuaries from you nor nobody else."

"Ah'll see she disnae!" roared Big Betty.

The floor shook as she rushed across to Rita.

"Ladies, ladies!" called Wee Andy. "Kindly do not let us have no unpreciadentit violence, if you please!"

But Rita was swinging her heavy shoulder bag at the onrushing dancer. With only a split second to spare, Wee Andy stepped back and emitted the low emergency whistle.

After being ejected by the henchmen with her usual level of struggle, Rita was charged with breach of the peace.

In court, she was still in a temper. "Ah never hut naebody!" she protested. Nevertheless, she was fined £3.

■ **Grand Surprise Floorshow**. You'd think the long-suffering patrons of the Okeydokey Club would have by now realised that any event promising any form of bright new talent was likely to end badly. Though perhaps that was the attraction!

■ **Rita the Critic**. This young lady is clearly on leave from her role teaching close-order fighting techniques to the SAS. Her combat skills, with almost any weapon that comes to hand, are quite incredible.

■ **Wee Andy M.C.** Why oh why does Andy persevere with his attempts to bring new acts to the OkeyDokey Club? It would seem that in the 30 years between 1950 and 1980 not a single one of the new acts has lived up to even half the magnitude of their billing. The reader could be forgiven for beginning to suspect that the Okeydokey Club might not be the world's greatest entertainment venue.

A kind act causes Senga tae come a cropper

SENGA had done an impulsive thing. She had bought a lounge suit at the sale for her husband, the middle-aged and pernickety Wee Stevie.

However, her kindness did not meet with the joyous reaction she had expected.

"Ye've went an' bought me a SUIT?" exclaimed the small gent. "Ye must be crackers! Ye know how partic'lar Ah am aboot choosin' ma claes".

"You shut yer face, ya ungrateful wretch!" requested the lady. "It's a luvly suit, a rale bargin. The man sayed it wiz an 'in' suit. 'Onybody who werrs that suit is 'with it', he sayed. Away n' pit it oan when Ah tell ye!"

With an extremely ill grace, Wee Stevie disappeared to attire himself in the up-to-date suit.

When he had wriggled his way into it his dismay was deeper than ever.

He stood before the wardrobe mirror, taking a critical look at how his suit hung upon him.

"Onybody who werrs this suit is 'with it', did you say?" he cried. "Naw, onybody who werrs this suit should huv his heid examin't!"

"Don't be stupit!" said Senga. "It fits perfect."

"Oh aye, it fits me like a glove," her husband assured her. "It's only got fower buttons on the front, nae lapels, an' it's waistit like a wumman's auld-fashint coastume!

"An its awfy bright, is it no? Whit is it, camel-coloured?"

"It's beige," came his wife's reply. "It's the way abody's suit will be coloured soon, the man told me. It's the new fashion."

It was clear that Wee Stevie's opinions on fashion ran somewhat at a tangent to the man who ran the clothing stall at the market and they were still discussing the merits of the ultra-modern creation, with continuing asperity, when Senga's younger sister, Diana, dropped in for a visit.

She was glad she had done so. At the first sight of her brother-in-law and his beige suit she burst into shrill peals of laughter.

"Aw, that's marvullus!" she yelled, only controlling her mirth with great difficulty. "Whit's he dressed up like that fur? Ur yiz gaun tae a fancy-dress dance or sump'n?"

Her sister and brother-in-law, their own argument put by for a second, looked at her stonily. No man or woman should interfere in another couple's argument.

But Diana was too carried away by her hilarity to notice the change in temperature, and continued, "Is he done up tae be the auldest Mod in Glesca!" she guffawed.

"Aw, an' the wee tight troosers is a panic! They make his wee legs look merr bandier than ever!"

"Naw, wait a minnit. Ah bought that suit fur him," said Senga. "It cost me five poun'."

"Aw, but it wiz worth it fur the laugh!" her sister burbled. "He parrylyses me!"

"AH'LL dae the parrylysin'," Senga roared angrily, and she gave her younger sister a resounding box on the ear.

"Whit did ye dae THAT fur?" asked Wee Stevie. "She's right aboot the suit. It makes me look like a dampt clown."

"Ye've AYE looked like a dampt clown!" bellowed the infuriated lady.

And she gave her spouse a thump on the face that sent him staggering back across the floor.

The resultant shouting and wailing, which went on at length, so alarmed the downstairs neighbours that the police were summoned.

Senga was charged with breach of the peace and assault.

"This is whit Ah get fur tryin' tae dae somebody a kindness!" she complained bitterly when the magistrate requested payment of £5.

■ **Ye must be crackers/You shut yer face.** I don't agree with you/Please stop talking. Terms of endearment in the Glesca patois. Husbands and wives sometimes show their affection in an oblique manner. It is a sign of how comfortable you are with your spouse if you can talk to them in such an unvarnished, plain-speech way. The shared love is sometimes difficult to detect beneath the robust terms of address a couple will employ when conversing, but it is always there.

■ **Waistit.** Waisted. How the garment is cut at the waist.

■ **Or sump'n.** Or something.

■ **Ur yiz gaun?** Are you two going? Yiz is usually a plural but can also be singular.

■ **Ma claes.** My clothes.

Table and chairs bargain costs Andra dear

MOIRA wasn't at all pleased when her husband, Andra, installed a tubular-legged table and four chairs to match in her kitchen.

"Whit wiz wrang wi' the widden table an' cherrs we've ariddy goat?" she asked him. "Whit did ye huv' tae go an' buy thae steel things fur?"

Andra was annoyed. "Whit ur ye haverin' aboot?" he barked. "Them steel-leggit cherrs an' the table is modern. An' besides, Ah goat a bargin' o' them. Three pun' fifteen fur the lot."

"Ah mighta knew!" scoffed the lady. "Wan o' yer stupit dampt bargins! Onybuddy wi' a bit o' rubbidge tae flog knows they've a mug oan the go when they see YOU comin'!"

"Whiddye mean by that?" cried Andra indignantly.

"Ye're aye bein' took in," Moira stated. "Look at that bargin shurt ye bought fur yoursel' fur fowerteen boab last week. It fell tae bits efter wan waashin', an' the purple dye oot it ruin't wan o' ma blouses."

"Well, the man in the shope sayed he'd chinge the shurt," said Andra.

"Aye, an' when ye went back wi the remains o' it the shop wiz closed up an' the mannie hud flew awa back tae Inglun'," his wife pointed out.

With ill grace she set the tea on the new table. But when she went to move the table the entire top came away and she was left holding it.

"Oh, the tap comes aff," exclaimed her husband admiringly. "Ye kin use it as a tray."

Moira gave him a pitying look. "The tap DOESNAE come aff it!" she rasped. "It's broke aff. It wiz jist pit oan tae the legs wi' thin solder!"

"You've went an' broke it, then!" alleged Andra. "That shows ye hoo haun'less ye ur. Nae wunner ma new shurt fell tae bits if that's the rough treatment ye gi'e things."

"Ah know a certain thing that's gonny get rough treatment if it doesnae cley up," said Moira menacingly.

"Gi'e us the tap o' the table an' Ah'll see if Ah kin fix it back oan," said Andra.

He took the laden table top and tried to stand it on the tubular legs. His wife shook her head sadly. "Aw, Ah gi'e up!" she sighed, and sat down on one of the new chairs.

Immediately there was a loud scream as the seat of the chair broke away from the legs. Moira's feet shot into the air as her substantial derrier plummeted to the floor.

"That cheap, rubbishy cherr collapsed the saicint Ah sat oan it!" she screamed as she scrambled to get to her feet.

"A wumman o' your weight's no' supposed tae hump hursel' doon oan it!" Andra told her.

The implication that she tended towards embonpoint was the last straw for Moira.

She picked up the seatless chair and banged it down on her husband's cranium. One of the legs snapped off.

"See, it even breks oan your big saft heid," she commented.

The rumpus that followed the chair-borne assault became so noisy that the police were summoned, and the couple were booked for disturbing the peace.

Andra was glum and silent in court.

Moira declared "It wiz a' his fault! If ever a wumman suffer't fae huvvin' a stupit man tae coantend wi', it's me!"

Then – "Pey ra fines," she ordered her husband when the magistrate requested £2 from each.

■ **Embonpoint.** Plumpness or fleshiness, especially with reference to a woman's bosom. Literally translated from French, "en bon point" means "in good condition".

■ **Three pun' fifteen.** £3.75.

■ **Fowerteen boab.** 70p.

■ **A mug oan the go.** A gullible purchaser on their hands. The bargain, the off-the-books transaction, the back-of-a-lorry purchase was always a beloved part of working class life. People wanted to get the most bang for their buck. Often the deal was a genuine bargain, even if the background and supply arrangements might not have stood up to the full glare of the law being shone upon them. But there were always sellers, or blokes in the pub, all too eager to take advantage of this love of a quick cash transaction. It took a customer with a discerning eye, or good luck, to differentiate between the genuine bargain and the fly man with a dodgy deal.

Jim's good deed lands him in the dog house

IT was a gay party, with young people standing about chatting animatedly holding drinks in their hands.

Little Rena, however, didn't know many of the guests, and she was standing looking rather lost in a corner.

Jim felt sorry for the small mouse-like girl, and he sauntered over to her. "Howya?" he said genially.

"Hello," said Little Rena without enthusiasm. "Can Ah get ye somethin' tae drink?" asked the gallant gent. The young lady shook her head.

"Oh, mibbe ye'd like a horse's doovur," said Jim. "Thur a hale tray o' them ower therr. Ah'll get a plate an' bring ye some."

"Please don't bother," Little Rena murmured.

Her small face held a strange expression and she suddenly blurted out, "Ah ruddy HATE that dame in the gold troosers! Ah hate hur! Ah hate hur! Ah HATE hur!"

The young lady who had roused these strong feelings was Big Joyce, a vivacious and curvaceous damsel who was dancing enthusiastically, and at several points in time with the beat, with a diminutive gent.

"Oh, ye mean ye've goat a notion o' Wee Sammy there?" Jim inquired of the small girl.

"Ah huvny goat a notion o' naebuddy! Ah jist want tae stand here and be all oan ma ain," snapped back Little Rena, with a look that said "daggers".

"Ye're makin' a mistake," said Jim. "Ah'll tell ye whit tae dae. Dance wi' me an' that'll make Wee Sammy jealous!"

Little Rena raked the gallant one with a scornful glare. "You fancy yer ruddy barra, ri' anough!" she exclaimed.

"D'ye think onybuddy wi' a face like yours could make ony guy jealous? Away an' gi'e me peace!"

Jim recoiled as if he'd been bitten by a cobra. "Aw ya bad-temper't little bizzim, ye!" he cried.

"Here Ah um tryin' tae help ye an' aw ye can dae is turn oan me an' insult me!"

"Ah don't want nae help fae the likes o' YOU" the small girl assured him.

"Don't worry!" cried Jim. "Ah'll no' try tae help ye again. Ah wiz jist sorry fur ye because ye wiz staunin' therr no' the size o' tuppence wi' yer face trippin' ye.

"Nae wunner Wee Sammy dizny fancy ye!"

This candid statement brought a shrill shriek of rage from Little Rena.

"Ya ugly-lookin' clown ye!" she yelled. "Ye look like somethin' that hud escaped oot the Addams Family!"

"Don't talk aboot onyone bein' ugly!" riposted Jim. "If Ah'd a face like yours, Ah'd be nasty-natturred an' a'."

Little Rena had no comment to make on this trenchant observation. She simply snatched up the tray of hors d'oeuvres and brought it down on the young gent's head with great force.

She was endeavouring to further indicate her low opinion of Jim by emptying a bowl of punch over his head when some of the other guests intervened.

In court next day, Little Rena was quite demure. "I think I must have took too many slugs oot of the punchboul," she explained primly.

She wasn't quite so prim when the magistrate fined her £5. "Aw zat no' ruddy sick'nin'!" she growled.

■ **Ah ruddy HATE that dame in the gold troosers**. I jolly well do not like that lady in the gold trousers. It has long been said that Glasgow is a town that is intrinsically no more violent or dangerous than any other city. No, the thing that marks Glasgow and Glaswegians as unusual is that a high proportion of its citizens are "gemme". Whereas any large connurbation has its thugs and gang members predisposed to physical violence, in Glasgow you'd be just as likely to experience fisticuffs from a wee wummin in a post office queue, a bus conductor, or the demure and benign-looking Little Rena, a seeming wallflower at an otherwise peaceable party. All Glaswegians are game for a fight if the occasion arises – a fact that should be remembered and respected by furriners.

■ **You fancy yer ruddy barra**. You, sir, clearly think you have a rather handsome face. There is a silent "In reality the reverse is the case" tacked on the end of this statement.

■ **Yer face trippin' ye**. Such a long-faced pout that you are in danger of falling over it.

■ **Zat no' ruddy sick'nin'**. I put it to you that this state of affairs would turn the stomach of any right-thinking person.

Wee Dan puts down the John Wayne of the cafe

THE cafe was well-filled with young ladies and gentlemen and the jukebox, in the language of the cognoscenti, was "gi'en it big licks."

Wee Danny, seated for the first time in his new girl friend Ella's favourite cafe, sipped his coffee and listened intently to various masterpieces of rock 'n' roll.

Then Big Lennie ambled in, his ample chest covered by a red polo-necked sweater.

He walked with a casual sway, the kind of perambulation affected by the film cowboy John Wayne when entering a saloon filled with hostile desperadoes.

"Who zis?" Wee Danny asked Ella. "The Sheriff o' Gallagate Creek?"

"Oh, here, don't let him see ye're lookin' at him!" whispered back the young lady.

"Wait a minnit!" said Wee Danny. "Whit's this we're getting'?"

"He's aye in here," whispered Ella. "An' naebuddy ever argues wi' him. He's a big fella, ye know."

"Oh, Ah see," murmured the small gent reflectively.

Then he lost interest in Big Lennie and once more bent an attentive ear to the jukebox.

Big Lennie lit a cigarette. From under lowered lids he surveyed the new gunslinger in town, Wee Danny.

The small gent did not notice. He was busy assisting the American maestro Buddy Holly from the jukebox with his cry of "Peggy Sue-ah! Peggy Sue-ah! Peggy-Peggy-Peggy-Peggy … Peggy Sue-ah!"

The record ended. Wee Danny turned to his girl-friend. "Rerr words tae that nummer, urn't they?" he said.

Ella did not answer. She was looking over his shoulder, an expression of fear on her face.

Wee Danny turned round and found himself looking up into the face of Big Lennie.

"Ah don't fancy the vocalisin', Mac," he said. "Naebuddy sings when Ah'm in this cafe, see?"

"Ah don't wonder at it," the small gent said calmly. "Ah wiz a bit depressed masel' when Ah seen ye comin' in."

Big Lennie breathed heavily. "Lissen, mister, you come outside," he growled.

"Naw, Ah huvny time, Mac," said the diminutive one.

"Ye're comin', mister," said the King of the Cafe. And he took hold of Wee Danny's tie.

Wee Danny's left fist travelled no more than ten inches before it jabbed his large adversary on the solar plexus.

Big Lennie was about to double up. Wee Danny, however, prevented this by giving him an uppercut with his right.

To the tune of "All Shook Up," Big Lennie measured his length on the floor.

There was some little confusion after that. Big Lennie was revived and Wee Danny was booked for assault.

In court, the small chap was eloquent in his own defence. "The big worknane thought he had me fur a mug," he explained to the magistrate.

The magistrate was obviously impressed. "Don't be too quick to take the law into your own hands," he told Wee Danny. "Off you go."

■ **Naebuddy sings when Ah'm in this cafe, see**. Big Lennie represents the local hard man. Most urban districts of any city would have one or two candidates for the title. The system remained based on the law of the playground, where the male hierarchy was decided on the grounds of physical size and that ill-defined concept "reputation". This was true of Glasgow, but also slightly different as this tale illustrates. As explained previously, the incredibly high proportion of "gemme" wee fellas in Glasgow meant the local hard nut could barely expect to go a full day without his status being challenged.

■ **Rerr**. Rare. The word retains its "uncommon" definition, as has passed into Anglish, to a degree. But the full meaning was more akin to "very good".

■ **John Wayne.** The western was the action movie of choice in the late 1950s when this tale is set. This was long before anyone had heard of comic book characters brought to life, kung fu exponents, or even James Bond and his many imitators. In any case, none of the later film heroes ever walked like Big John walked.

■ **Don't be too quick to take the law into your own hands.** No fine or other sentence was passed. Laying out well-built John Wayne imitators who wanted to "take you outside" was clearly regarded as fair play.

Flare-up when Uncle fan gets flattened

D ANNY plonked himself down in front of the television set. He warned his wife, Ethel – "Noo, don't say nuthin' while ma programme's oan."

He was sitting forward on his chair eagerly watching the machinations of the supermen and villains in The Man From U.N.C.L.E. when the doorbell rang.

A few seconds later Ethel was ushering her friend, Big Nora, into the room.

"Well, how are ye gettin' oan?" the large lady, in her hearty way, asked Ethel.

"Ah huvny saw ye since the menaudge fund dance," Nora went on. "Did ye manidge tae get his loardship here sober in time fur his work nixt moarnin'?"

"Aw, gi'e us a brek!" protested Danny, not wanting his performance at the dance discussed, or his TV viewing interrupted. "Gi'e us a BREK!"

"Aw, don't deny it noo!" cried Big Nora. "Ye hud goat a guid bucket in ye at the dance!"

"That's no' whit's worryin' him," said Ethel. "It's The Man fae Uncle."

"Oh right, kin he no' get his watch oot o' the pawn again?" asked the guest.

"Naw, naw, no' THAT uncle," explained Ethel. "It's that thing oan the TV therr. Ye know, Illya Kurywhitnutt an' Napoleon Soda an' spies an rat."

"But that's a TV show fur WEANS!" Big Nora explained. "It's a' shootin' an' death rays an' that."

"He dizny like tae miss ony of this programme," Ethel informed the large lady.

"Shut it!" roared the U.N.C.L.E. fan. "Ye've went an' made me miss whit the lassie wiz sayin' tae Napoleon!"

"Oh, ah see. He's goat his eye oan the blonde nixt," said Big Nora. "Ma man's the same, of course. There's a big blonde in The Newcomers he's aye gapin' at. Men's a' the same. Stupit numbskulls."

"Aye, well. They seem tae be awfy fond o' blonde hair," conceded Ethel.

"We'll huv tae stert dyein' wir herr," Big Nora cried, and

dissolved into loud and enthusiastic guffaws at her own witty observations.

"You can stert dyin' as quickly as ye can as faur as Ah'm coancern't," Danny barked at her. "It's a blinkin' shame! Ah'm sittin' lookin' at the wan programme thut Ah like oan ra tillyvision, an' then YOU huv tae come in wi' yer big fat mooth gaun' like the clappers!"

Nora's humour came to a sudden halt. "Oh, so Ah've a big mooth, huv Ah?" said the large lady.

"Aye, ye dae. Look in a mirror if ye waant tae check. Now stoap talkin' till Ah see hoo Illya gets oota this trap!" commanded the gent.

"Ah'm only interestit in WAN trap!" Big Nora shouted. "An' Ah'm gonna close it right now!"

With this, she emulated the violence on the screen by swinging her fist and knocking the gent off his chair. Her attack didn't stop there, and she began aiming further blows at Danny with her handbag.

Ethel, alarmed by the contretemps, and possibly frightened for her husband's wellbeing, summoned the police. Big Nora was subdued and escorted cell-wards.

In court on an assault charge the next day, she apologised. "Ah loast ma temper," she admitted. "Ah loss ma temper easy wi' stupit men." The magistrate intimated she would also lose £5.

■ **Menaudge fund.** A menage fund could be a type of prize draw, in which many would contribute a few pennies over the course of weeks or months, then a name was selected by lot to decide who got the lump sum. It could also be a savings fund in which money would be paid in, then withdrawn when enough had accumulated for a large purchase such as a three-piece suit or a bicycle.

■ **Gi'e us a brek.** Give me a break. Give me a rest. This was a common plea in the middle decades of the 20th Century, but has somewhat passed out of usage. Interestingly, the "us" can equally mean "us" plural, or "I", singular, or both at the same time.

■ **The Man fae Uncle.** Popular TV show The Man From U.N.C.L.E. featured unlikely events acted out by good looking young chaps pretending to be USSR and USA secret agents.

■ **Gaun' like the clappers.** Going like the clappers. This is a Glesca pronunciation of the old military slang term. In the original saying, the clappers referred to were within "hell's bells".

Bill and Frank's Uncle-inspired dame-attracting plan goes awry

B IG Bill and Wee Frank were plodding along the street together when the small chap became aware of the fact that his large crony was studying him with some intensity.

"Whit the divvle ur ye sterrin at me fur?" he asked. "Huv' Ah got durt oan ma face or sump'n'?"

"Naw, naw," said Big Bill. "It's no' that – Heh, d' you realise that ye look a bit like Eela Cooryakin?"

"Ye mean the fella in 'The Man from Uncle'?" asked Wee Frank. "Ye're kiddin'!"

"Naw, ri' anough," insisted the big chap. "Ye've got the same kinna light-colour't eyes an' the same sticky-oot forehead. If yer herr wiz brushed furrit, ye could be his double."

"Oh, Ah could easy brush it furrit," said Wee Frank quickly, quite taken with the notion.

"Ah, but Eela Cooryakin's herr is merr lighter than yours," Big Bill told him.

"Izzit?" said his crony. He pondered, then – "Ye know, Ah could lighten it a wee bit. The sister's got stuff for that. Ah could borra a wee bit."

"Goash, ye'd get the burds runnin' efter ye like mad if ye looked like Eela Cooryakin!" Big Bill assured him.

So, assisted by his sister, the small chap bleached his hair in front and brushed it forward in the style of The Man from U.N.C.L.E. star.

Upon conclusion of this cosmetic work, the pair were highly pleased with the results. "It's fabyullus!" enthused Big Bill. "It's jist a peety Ah don't look like Napoleon Solo."

"Ah think we'll dae a' right wi' ma new Cooryakin immidge," said Wee Frank modestly. An hour later they were on their way to the dancing.

But, even when they joined two acquaintances Chrissie and Janice, who had been given ample chance to get a good look at the aspiring action hero, there was no mention of the inclusion of Mr Kuryakin in the party.

Instead, Janice asked Wee Frank, "Whit huv ye went an' did tae yer herr?"

"He's went white in wan night!" laughed Chrissie. "Did ye get an awfy fright or sumpin'? Oh, that hauf-blonde, hauf-mousy broon style looks right coamical!"

"Naw, naw. Ye're no' gettin' it. Does he no' make ye think o' somebody oan the TV?" prompted Big Bill.

The young ladies pondered. "Surely ye don't mean Kathy Kirby? I see it noo!" gasped Chrissie with mock astonishment.

"Aw, don't try tae be funny," growled Wee Frank.

His big crony persevered. "Look, huv ye never watched The Man from Uncle?" he asked the damsels. "He's like somebody in IT!"

"Naw, he's merr liker somethin' oota Dr Who!" said Janice. "Wan o' the monsters, like."

"Aw wait, AH gerrit!" cried Chrissie. "It IS Kathy Kirby he's tryin' to make hissel' look like! Gie's a song, go'wan. Goan dae the Calamity Jane wan."

The young ladies laughed uproariously.

"It'll no' dae pal," said Janice. "Wee smouts like you is jist no' the Carnaby Street type."

"Don't talk about ME bein' a wee smout!" said the small chap angrily. "Bowlly-leggit wee scunners like you shouldny critycise onybody!"

Janice's reply to this was a screech of rage.

As she launched herself at the pseudo Kuryakin she was restrained by Big Bill. He put his hand on her face and pushed her back the way she had come.

This laying on of hands led to his appearance in court next day on an assault charge.

"He shoulda went tae the dancin' as a dampt Dalek," he muttered as he paid his £4 fine.

■ **Durt**. There is a richness of meaning and an almost delicious pleasure in pronouncing "durrrt" in Glaswegian, that elevates the word to a new level of durtyness that is altogether lacking in any accent that doesn't have the extravagantly rolled Scots Rs.

■ **Eela Kuryakin**. Illya Kuryakin, the Soviet half of the fictional international espionage U.N.C.L.E team was played by Maryhill-born actor David McCallum. He was regarded as a sex symbol throughout the show's 1964-68 run and any man would have been pleased to be compared to him.

■ **Kathy Kirby**. Platinum blond singer, the UK's answer to Marilyn Monroe, who represented the UK at the 1965 Eurovision Song Competition.

A long-haired nyuck gets warrior Willie short-tempered

WILLIE gave an exclamation of amazement when he walked into the kitchen and caught sight of his niece, Shirley.

"Well, Ah'll be dampt!" he cried. "Ye're readin' a newspaper. Ah've never saw ye daen' THAT afore! Or ur ye jist lookin' at the photies in it?"

The sultry-looking young lady gave her uncle a brief bleak look. "Ah'm readin' aboot The Beatles, if ye want tae know," she informed him.

"Oh, it wid huv tae be be aboot THEM!" said Willie. "Ah widna catch ye readin' anything' aboot Harold Wilson or Edward Heath, widda?"

"Never heard o' them," stated Shirley. "Dae they play wi' a group, or sump'n?"

"Oh, hivven help us!" her uncle sighed. "Ye've nae interest in important things at a'!"

He opened his own newspaper and began a serious study of the football results and treble chance forecasts.

"Heh," said Shirley, "You don't like boys wi' long herr, sure ye don't?"

"Naw!" growled Willie, deep in his research on the chances of Stranraer recording a draw against Cowdenbeath.

"Well here, lissen tae whit it says in this paper about boys wi' long herr," she said. "It says – 'They represent a clean break with the ault-fashion't past in favour of a modern dynamic trend'."

Her uncle, who listened to this with his mouth agape, threw down his paper.

"Ah see," he said. "Yer sayin' thae young nyucks that looks like lassies is dynamic, an' us short-herred yins that done wur stuff at El Alamein WIZNY dynamic, izzat it?"

"Aw, don't gi'e us the his'try o' how you won the war again," said Shirley wearily. "Ye're just jealous o' the young fellas wi' thur luvly long herr because ye've went baldy."

"It wiz the steel helmet Ah wore when Ah wiz fightin' fur you an' yer dynamicky herry pals that made me go baldy!" exploded the former warrior.

He was still ranting on, with assorted references to shrapnel and panzer divisions, when Shirley went to the door to admit her boy friend, Tony.

It transpired that he had just come from the hairdresser's.

"Jings, Ah wiz ages sittin' under the dryer therr," he told Shirley.

Willie shook his head uncomprehendingly that a man should spend time under a dryer having his hair set. Then he said to Tony, "An' ah suppose you'll be wan o' these dynamic wans I'm hearin' aboot, eh?"

"Ah don't dig ye, Mac," the long-haired young gent said, somewhat confused.

"Look," said Willie, "when Ah wiz your age ma herr wiz cut short, an' Ah looked like a man."

"Aw, well appearances can be deceptive, like," retorted Tony.

"Whit d'ye mean by that?" asked the older gent angrily. His question went unanswered as Tony and Shirley were laughing gaily at the quip.

"He diznae gerrit!" guffawed the young gent. "Oh, he's no' a squerr, this yin – he's a cube!" cried Shirley. "He wiz tellin' me whit he done at El Alamein."

"Whit's that?" asked the dynamic youth. "Is it a club in the toon?" Further laughter ensued.

This disrespect was the last straw for the desert war veteran.

"Never heard o' whit we did at El Alamein!" he cried. "We're the reason you kin sit an hiv yer hair done up like a carnation. Ya mug, Ah'll flatten ye!"

He thereupon gave Tony a thump on the head that jolted his newly-baked coiffure to its foundations.

Willie's regrettable loss of control led to his first-ever appearance in court.

The war hero was profuse in his thanks when the magistrate put him on probation for one month.

■ **Harold Wilson and Edward Heath**. A comedy duo of the era, though some of their more famous routines, "Austerity measures" and "The three-day week" were often difficult to laugh at.

■ **The Battles of El Alamein**. A British Army-Afrika Korps fixture of 1942, some 30 years previous to when this tale is set. A narrow win for the UK lads over two legs. And, it must be said, a thirst-ravaged, shrapnel-blasted, bullet-ridden hell-on-earth.

Hot time at the dancin' when wee Frank plays it cool

WEE Frank was particularly impressed by the James Bond film he and Big Bill had just seen.

"Did ye notice how Bond huz a' thae marvullus-lookin' burds chasin' efter him?" the small gent asked his crony.

"D'ye know whit his secret is? He smokes special fags, knows a' aboot foreign food an' wine, an' furby a' that, he's goat an aroma o' mystery aboot him."

"Zat whit makes the burds go fur him in a big way?" asked Big Bill, hanging on every word.

"Aye! Of course it is!" the small chap assured him. "Whit WE want tae dae is tae gi'e wursels the James Bond immidge. An' Ah know how tae dae it."

Soon he was indoctrinating his big crony with Bond-ism. Three evenings later, thoroughly versed in the sophisticated idiosyncrasies of the celebrated hero-figure, the gents set off for the dancing.

They were wearing dark suits and ties, smoking French cigarettes, and Wee Frank sported a pair of dark glasses.

"They make me look mysterious," he explained.

"Ah shoulda pit oan mines, then," said Big Bill.

"That widda been too much – baith o' us in dark glesses," said the Bond expert. "Besides, you've goat oan the rid waistcoat."

They weren't long in the dance hall before they caught sight of two prepossessing damsels.

"Aw, now therra perra dolls!" exclaimed Big Bill excitedly.

"Aye. So play it cool, play it COOL," said Wee Frank. "First of a' we light up a couple o' wur French fags."

"Here, Ah'll feel stupit gaun' ower wi' a couple fags in ma mooth," said Big Bill. "Ur ye sure James Bond –"

"We EACH light up a fag, ya mug ye!" rasped the small chap irascibly. "Hurry up an' light up! Right. Now, we'll saunter ower tae them. Casual-like."

So they sauntered, with much casualness, over to the young ladies. "Hello there laydeesh," said Wee Frank in simple, matter-of-fact, James Bond style.

It soon became apparent that the young ladies did not perceive any likeness in the cronies to 007 secret agents.

"Oh, goash, we thought yiz wiz a coupla undertakers comin' tae get us!" laughed Anne, a pert blonde.

Her friend Janice was too concerned to be amused. "Hey, thur sump'n burnin'!" she cried, sniffing the air and looking round for the nearest fire exit.

"Naw, it's thur FAGS!" Anne pointed out shrilly. "Whit is that ye're smokin' – aul' rags?"

"Naw, thems urr French," explained Wee Frank, holding up his odd-smelling cigarette for examination. "We always smoke French cigarettes, see." And, to add further colour to his romantic, Bond-like image, he added, "Aye, and we always drink the wine, too."

"Oh, jings, a coupla wineys!" exclaimed Anne. "Youse is gonny be in a bonnie mess afore long wi' yer taury-rope fags an' yer rid biddy!"

When the young ladies declined the offer of French cigarettes and elected to smoke their own previously stubbed cigarettes, Wee Frank whipped out his gas cigarette lighter with true Bond-style alacrity.

Unfortunately, he hadn't adjusted it properly and a four-inch jet of flame shot out.

A loud screech came from Anne as she clutched her nose.

Wee Frank gazed at her unperturbably. "I am afraid your dout was too small," he said suavely.

Anne, in pain and infuriated, swept up a glass ashtray from a nearby table with the obvious intention of bringing it down on the small chap's skull.

Big Bill prevented this by stepping in to give her a clout on the countenance. This defensive measure led to his appearance in court on an assault charge.

Fined £3 he made a most un-Bond-like remark. "Ah'm beginnin' tae hate the sight o' burds!" he growled.

■ **Taury-rope**. A tarry rope. French cigarettes of the 1960s had, it must be said, a quite different aroma to the normal British tobacco product. To compare the smell to a tarry rope is very much a sign that young Miss Anne wasn't impressed.

■ **Dout**. A half-smoked cigarette. Might also be known as a dowp, or a stub.

■ **Burds**. Birds. Women, especially young attractive women. A term only ever used by men.

Dinner-suited Sanny turns a dance intae a disaster

SANNY was considerably discomfited when he arrived with his wife, May, at the private dance, and found that he was the only gent present wearing a dinner suit.

"Hivvins, they're a' in oardinary suits!" he exclaimed. "An' here um Ah in this hired outfit. Whit did you say they'd all be in denner jaickits fur?"

"Ach, stoap mumpin'," said May. "That denner suit jist aboot does the impoassible fur you. Ye almost look like a gentleman werrin' it."

"It makes me look like a dampt idiot!" retorted Sanny. "An' it's costin' me thurty-five boab, tae. An' look at the troosers – faur too wide. The jaickit's too –"

His stream of complaints was interrupted by a small gent who approached, and said urgently, "Coarnur table owrerr, Mac. Five wee whiskies, two gin an' toanics an' a boattla beer."

Then, leaving Sanny open-mouthed with shock, he hurried back to his friends. "In the name o' hivvin!" gasped the dinner-suited one, "he thinks Ah'm a dampt waiter!"

"Never mind," said May, "thur nae shame in bein' mistook fur a waiter, ye know. You're that thin-skinn't. Ye should . . ." But her husband had been buttonholed by a large lady.

"Excuse me," she said. And she whispered into his ear.

Sanny was appalled. "Ah've nae idea whaur the powder-room is!" he told her.

"Oh, some manager you are!" expostulated the large lady. "Too big in the heid tae help orrinary folks, ur ye? Weel, as faur as Ah'm coancern't ye're just a ruddy flunkey. Ye kin stick yer dinner-dance."

May tried to explain. "Naw, he's ma man, no a . . . " she began.

"Ah don't cerr WHOSE man he is!" bellowed the disgruntled guest. "Ah asked him a civil question, an' it's his joab tae gi'e me a civil answer!"

By this time Sanny was breathing heavily with frustration. "Will ye lissen tae me?" he said to the large lady. "Ah'm here as wan o' the guests, an' Ah'm no' a . . . "

"Heh, mac, whirraboot thae drinks?" said a voice at his elbow. The small thirsty gent had returned.

"Drinks?" echoed Sanny blankly, turning to him.

"Aw, wake up, man!" barked the small gent angrily. "Ah ordered five wee whiskies, two gin-an' toanics, an' a boattla beer. That wiz ten minnits ago, an' Ah'm still waitin'!"

"Ah canny help THAT!" exploded Sanny.

"He canny help NAE-buddy!" put in the large lady, who was still present..

"He's too busy staunin' aboot gassin' tae dae ony work, it seems," declared the small gent.

"Aye, dress them up in a fancy suit an' they get too big fur thur boots," the large lady complained. "Gentleman Jim, here, disnae WAANT tae work."

"Aw, shut yer face!" cried Sanny, losing the will to explain any further.

"Don't loss yer temper, Sanny," warned May.

"It's ME that's gonny loss ma temper if he disnae bring thae drinks tae ma table right away!" proclaimed the small gent. And he put his angry face close to Sanny's.

The exasperated gent in the dinner jacket brought his open hand down on it with some force.

The tragedy of errors ended in court when Sanny was fined £5 for assault.

"By jings, it's cost me nearly a tenner tae attend that disaster o' a dance!" he cried as he paid his fine.

■ **Stoap mumpin'; staunin' aboot gassin'; whirraboot thae drinks; disnae waant tae work.** All standard phrases in the Glasgow dialect which should be mastered by any tourist who wishes a fully immersive experience in the culture. As ever, the phrases should be delivered with a degree of vehemence. This isn't a language that suits modulated tones or dulled-down delivery. Glaswegian is a world-leading example of a method of communication that combines base meaning with style to mean much more than the simple words on their own can say. It is how you say it, as well as what you say, that makes it such a remarkable anthropological study.

■ **Only gent in a dinner suit.** The type of suit worn to occasions such as a dinner-dance was a much more important issue in the 1960s and '70s than it is now that "smart casual" dress is all that is usually required for any occasion. A 1960s faux-pas such as the wrong sort of suit would mark the wearer out as not being a member of the cognoscenti (the people who know) or (see above) as a waiter.

Big Bill's barney with a horse fancier

THERE was a certain wariness in Big Bill's expression when Wee Frank told him excitedly that he had arranged a Saturday afternoon outing for the two of them. "Who's the burds an' whit's it gonny cost us?" asked the big chap guardedly.

"Aw, don't be like that!" said Wee Frank. "We're in among the Class noo. Ye know how you're aye sayin' ye're fed up lumberin' dames that's jist scruff. Well, Sybil an' Lesley's diff'rint."

"D'ye mean them two burds ye wiz chattin' up when Ah came inty the coacktail lounge last Friday?" queried Big Bill.

"Aye, Ah thought we might date them up," explained the small gent. "An' Ah've did it! Ye'll never guess whaur we're gaun'!"

"Tae some fancy joint wherr they'll eat an' drink so much we'll be skinn't fur a month," muttered Big Bill lugubriously.

"Aw, hivvins, you're a right mizzenthorpe!" said Wee Frank impatiently. "We're no' gaun' tae nae fancy joint. We're gaun' up tae a farm in Lesley's shootin' brake tae see Lesley's hoarse!"

"That's a funny way o' spendin' a Setterday efternin," said his larger crony.

"Whit ur ye talkin' aboot?" Wee Frank snapped. "Here's two classy burds ready tae take ye inty the country in thur caur an' you're raisin' oabjectshuns!"

"Naw, naw," said Big Bill. "Ah wiz jist wonderin' whit we'd dae efter we'd looked at the hoarse."

"Aw, well," said the small chap. "There's a hangava good wee hotel oot there where we could take Sybil an' Lesley fur a meal.

"Aw, ye waant tae see them in thur jodpurrs!" he went on. "Ah seen a photy o' them. Oh, do thae two burds look cool!"

"'Zatso?" commented Big Bill, with rapidly heightening interest. "Here, lissen, we better pit oan the sports jaickets an' wur Chelsea boots. Ah've goat mine's poalished up so's ye kin see yer face in them."

But there was a twinge of disappointment when the young ladies picked them up in their vehicle the following day.

The shooting brake turned out to be a small and ancient van, the back of which was filled with straw, old buckets, an antique saddle, and other equine bric-a-brac.

"You cheps'll hev to crush in there on top of thet stuff," said Sybil in the strange, strangled accent formed by so many of the young ladies who inhabit Glasgow's suburbia.

After a very uncomfortable thirty minutes, the party arrived at the farm. "Here we are," said Lesley. "Would you two mind bringing some of that bedding?"

The two young ladies then filled the arms of their horrified escorts with straw. "Off we go!" said Sybil briskly. "The stable's just over here."

The horsewomen, clad not in smart jodhpurs but in shapeless sweaters, faded denims, and wellingtons, led the way across a morass of noisome farmyard mud.

"This is a dampt impusition!" growled Big Bill to his crony. "Ma Chelsea boots is ruin't! An' look at yer classy dames. A perra bloomin' horrurs!"

"Come on, you chaps!" called Lesley. "The big boy's waiting to be groomed."

"It's no' the hoarse that needs groomin'," muttered Big Bill, squelching towards the stable with his load.

There was only room for the two equestriennes and the horse in the small stall. The cronies had to wait outside in the chill rain.

Two miserable hours later the quartet were on their way back to the city. Wee Frank had thought better of inviting the young ladies for a meal. When they dropped their escorts in the city, Lesley said candidly to the cronies, "Well, Ai must say you heven't been awfleh laively company!"

"Nae wunner," said Wee Frank. "We're no' yased tae lumberin' a couple borin' bumpkins."

Lesley turned to Sybil. "Whai do you always seem to mix with the wrong people?" she asked.

"A deshed stupid mistake!" admitted Sybil.

To emphasise her point she leaned from the van and aimed a blow at Wee Frank with the grooming brush.

Big Bill thwarted her by pushing her face back into the interior of the van. Screeches from the two young ladies brought the police to the scene.

Bill was charged with assault. "Anything to say?" he was asked in court. "Seein' Ah'm a dunkey, Ah'll say hee-haw," he retorted. Glumly he stumped up the £7 fine.

■ **Mizzenthorpe**. Misanthrope. A person who dislikes all humankind. This is an impressive addition to Wee Frank's vocabulary, he has obviously been reading the magazines in the dentist's waiting room.

■ **You cheps. Laively. Deshed.** The perils of the class divide. As all Glaswegians know, people from the suburbs talk funny and act funny. None of them can be trusted. Anyone who canna prenunce their wurdz proaperly is a bampoat.

'Dr Crippen' Sam springs a surprise at social club do

THE street's annual social club dance was due that evening, and an air of pleasant anticipation pervaded the community.

Meg and Caroline, two young ladies scheduled to attend, met in the street by chance that morning.

"Oh, here, thur somethin' diff'rint aboot you!" exclaimed Caroline, eyeing the other keenly. "Oh, Ah KNOW whit it is. Ye've went an' washed yer heid-scarf!"

"Ah hope you're gonny waash yer herr afore the night," retorted Meg, with a scornful glance at the other maiden's long straight tresses.

"Don't worry," said Caroline, "Ah'll huv ma herr did. An' it'll no' be a' in crimpy wee imytation waves like yours. You want tae get with it an' no' go aboot lookin' like some aul'-fashint dame oota Dr Finlay's Casebook."

"Away an' get raffle't!" riposted Meg, as the two young ladies parted on bad terms.

That evening they met face to face on the dance floor. Meg's hair WAS in crimpy little waves, and was sprinkled with powder that made it glitter. Her ballerina dress was adorned with sequins.

"Oh, it's Fairy Slush!" exclaimed Caroline, who, in her trend-setting way, was dressed in a shapeless jumper and very short skirt, which set off her heavily-decorated stockings.

"Wid ye look at who's makin' cracks aboot me!" shrilled Meg to her partner. "Fancy onybody like hur werrin' a shoart skirt an' fancy stoackins! They make her legs look like a perra pillars that's collapsin'."

"Away ye go, ya stupit-lookin' squerr, ye!" Caroline raged. "Ye're behind the times. Away an' dance the auld-fashint waltz wi' wee Doactur Crippen there."

The gentleman referred to was Meg's partner, Sam, a diminutive individual with spectacles and a small, black moustache.

"Iggerant toerag!" roared Meg. "Ah've a guid mind tae belt the dial aff ye!"

At this warlike manifestation, Caroline's partner, Big Harry, stepped forward. "Whissamarrer? Whissamarrer?" he growled.

Sam nodded at Caroline. "Take this person away before I forget I'm a gentleman and tell her what I think of her," he fluted in a squeaky voice.

"Don't hit him, Sam," pleaded Meg.

Caroline laughed shrilly. "Oh, wid ye lissen tae that. She's tellin' him no' tae hit ye, Harry!"

"Aye, Ah heard her." Growled the big chap. Then he swung his huge, ham-like fist at Sam's face.

In an almost simultaneous moment, the small gent removed his spectacles, put them in his breast pocket, dodged the fist and planted a haymaker on Big Harry's jaw.

Caroline gave a cry of mingled astonishment and fear as her beefy partner went down with a tremendous crash.

Sam went off peaceably with two constables who were called to the scene.

In court he admitted the assault. "I'm afraid I had to do it," he squeaked in apology.

It turned out he'd never before been in trouble with the law.

"Oh, Sam!" called Meg adoringly as her small hero was admonished.

■ **Aul'-fashint dame oota Dr Finlay's Casebook**. A TV series that ran from 1962 to 1971, but was set in the 1930s. In the fashion-conscious 1960s, to be accused of wearing pre-war clothes would be a withering insult. How people looked was becoming an ever-more-important part of the social make-up of the nation. Both men's (see previous court case) and women's fashions were becoming more marked and were changing ever faster.

■ **Trendy short skirt**. The mini-skirt was, by the mid-1960s regarded as the most fashionable, most daring female outfit. It represented the "swinging sixties" more than any other garment. Often, in those early days, worn with extravagantly-patterned or harlequin-patterned tights. Mary Quant, one of several possible inventors of the mini-skirt, was quoted as saying the mini was worn by young, active women who didn't want to resemble their mothers. However, as Meg points out above, a mini-skirt wearer had to have legs that benefited from being exposed.

■ **Doactur Crippen**. Legendary wife-murderer Dr Hawley Harvey Crippen had been hanged for his crimes in 1910, although his lover, Ethel Le Neve, lived until 1967. But Crippen's dread shadow clearly still fell on 1960s society. To be compared to this slight, bespectacled, moustachioed bogeyman was another deadly insult.

A pie and peas order lands waitress Margaret in a pickle

IT had been a long and busy day for Margaret, the waitress in the small tearoom. Thankfully, she noted that the establishment was empty, and slumped down on a chair. "Aw, ma feet's killin' me!" she observed to another weary waitress.

"Ah hope naebuddy else comes in. Ah'm seeck tae daith o' watchin' folk feedin' thur faces."

No sooner had the words left her mouth than Jerry and his decorative girl friend, Anne, sauntered through the doorway and sat at a table.

"Aw, ta hang!" growled Margaret, slowly hoisting herself to her feet and shuffling slowly over to the table.

"Whiddjizwaant?" she asked.

Margaret received a shock when the young gent looked up and she saw he was a boy friend from whom she had parted, with not a little acrimony, a year or so before.

"Oh, goash!" Jerry exclaimed. "Fancy seein' you daen' yer waitressin' . . ."

Anne, Jerry's accompanying blonde, now butted in. "Heh, whirraboot somethin' tae eat?" she said in a metallic voice.

Jerry turned to her with alacrity and concern. "Oh, Ah'm terrible sorry!" he said. "Therr the menu. Huv onythin' ye see."

"Huh, you're a oaptymist!" muttered Margaret. "Thur no' much left oan the menu."

"Thur plenty o' greasy spoats oan it," commented Anne sourly.

Her eye went to the costliest item on the card. "Whirraboot the breist o' chicken?" she said.

"Aye, huv rat!" Jerry told her eagerly.

"Breist o' chicken?" muttered the waitress. "Ye're ferrly lashin' the dough aboot NOO. Ah wiz lucky if Ah goat a tanner poke o' chips."

"Breist o' chicken fur two," said the young gent grandly. "An' French-fried potatoes."

"Sorry, Mr Onassius, the chicken's aff, an' so's the potatoes," Margaret intimated with ill-concealed relish.

The blonde sighed. "Bring me two pies an' pit plenty peas oan tap o' them." Her escort signified that he would have the same, and Margaret sauntered off.

"Two double pie and peas," she called to someone behind the scenes.

Fully fifteen minutes elapsed before she returned to the table with the repasts. Anne was far from pleased. "It took ye a long time," she told the waitress. "An' izzat a' ra peas we're gettin'? Thur just five oan tap o' the pies."

That's a' the peas that's left," Margaret informed her. "An' ye better get yer pies ett up quick. We're shuttin' in five minutes."

"Ta hang wi' THAT!" exploded the blonde. "We've been waitin' a' this time an' ye expect us tae scoaff two pies in five minutes."

"Wi' a mooth the size o' yours ye'll get them doon ye in five saicints," observed Margaret, taking off her apron.

"Heh, that's anuffa RAT!" protested Jerry.

"We'll no' eat hur rotten pies at a'!" cried the blonde. "An' we'll no' pey nuthin', neether! Come oan!"

But before she could rise she was pushed back into her chair by the waitress.

Anne's blonde hair then assumed a variegated hue as Margaret snatched up one of the pies and slammed it down on top of her coiffure.

Wild screeching filled the air. Soon the police were on the scene and Margaret was booked for assault.

"Ah wiz takin' the pie away when she jiggle't ma erm an' it fell oan her heid," she told the magistrate.

The learned gentleman chose not believe her. A loud wail escaped Margaret when she was instructed to disburse £3.

■ **Mr Onassius**. A reference to the luxurious spending power of Aristotle Onassis, the go-to comparator for 1960s opulence.

■ **Whiddjizwaant?** What would you like from the menu? The running-together of words is reminiscent of the Germanic roots of the language — a linguistic tradition often at the forefront of Glesca cafe waitresses' thoughts.

■ **Izzat a' ra peas?** Is that all the peas? The phrase forms a challenge in the guise of a question. It implies a lack of value for money, laced with accusatory tones. When you've requested peas with your pie, you have every right to expect a reasonable amount of peas.

■ **Jiggle't ma erm.** Jogged my arm. There is more action, more movement, more cause to coup a plate of pie and peas on to someone's head, contained in jiggle't than in jogged — hence Margaret's choice of term.

A barney when Auld Boab shatters love's young dream

L OVE was in the air. Lorna and Gregor, the young gent she intended to marry, were alone and seated on a couch in the front room of her abode.

Gregor turned, sighed, and directed a loving look at his inamorata.

He was about to whisper a selection of romantic nothings into her ear when the door opened and Lorna's grandfather, Auld Boab, walked in. "Aw, thae tillyvision programmes wid seecken ye, so thae wid!" declared the ancient one, plumping himself down in a chair.

"Ah'm no' sittin' in that kitchen watchin' a perra eedjits kissin' wan anither an' talkin' a lot o' noansense!"

"It's the play," said Lorna. "It'll be feenished soon."

"WHIT'LL be feenished soon?" asked Auld Boab, cupping his hand round an ear. "Ah'm no' feenished YIT, ye know. It's only them that's in thur dotage that sits an' watches that dampt tillyvision!"

"Aye, aye, sure," said Gregor. "But is it no' the fitba' that's oan the TV noo?"

This distraction tactic, however, failed to work.

"Naw, thur nae fitba' oan the night," the old gent told him. "Nuthin' but lassies gi'en men the glad eye an' huggin' an' kissin'. It's a disgrace! In ma young days we didnae huv tae sit an' watch that kinna thing."

"Aye, but naebuddy's askin' ye tae watch it," Lorna shouted into his ear. She had another idea. "Could you no go away tae yer scratcher an' read a book?" she asked.

Auld Boab glared at her. "That book yer maw brung me fae the liberry?" he asked. "It's a scandal! A' aboot a man leavin' his wife, n' coortin' anither lassie. An' it goes oan like that right tae the very last page!"

And on and on he went with his tirade against TV plays, modern youth, the lack of chastity in literature, and other scandalous present-day phenomena. It hadn't been like this during the war. They'd only had national brid tae eat. It was all Edvis Presser's fault, or possibly Frank Sinitata. Or both.

As he sat bored to tears at the never-ending, rarely accurate, and wholly unsubstantiated list of grievances, Gregor put his hand round Lorna's waist. She, in return, returned to gazing fondly into his face.

Auld Boab perceived this, and was appalled. "In the name o' hivvin'!" he cried. "Whit kinna wey is that tae cairry oan furnenst onybody? As if we don't see anough o' shameless canoodlin' oan the tillyvision!"

Gregor unhanded the maiden and sat forward on his seat so that his face was close to that of the old gent.

"Aw fur Pete's sake!" he exclaimed heatedly. "Wull ye shut yer stupid aul' geggie an' go away an' leave us in peace?"

At this request, Auld Boab displayed remarkable agility for a man of his years.

Grabbing up his stout walking stick that stood in a corner, he brought it down with a resounding crack on Gregor's cranium. "That'll mibbe learn ye some manners, ya tuppence-hap'ny Casanovia, ye!" he cried.

Gregor did not hear much of this. He slumped back on the couch, stunned.

"Ya auld hoodlum, ye!" screeched Lorna. "Gi'e us that stick."

Boab did as he was bid and gave her the stick – also aimed at her forehead.

The downstairs neighbours, worried by the noise and screeches, summoned Her Majesty's constabulary forthwith.

The aged recalcitrant was removed and subsequently charged with assault.

"Ah wiz insultit," he quavered in court, and started again to list his grievances.

The magistrate ordered silence, gave him a strongly-worded dressing-down, and put him on probation for three months.

■ **Seecken ye, so thae wid**. Sicken you, so they would. An intensifier. It was common to add "so thae wid", "wid it no", "right eenuff" or other phrase on the end of a sentence to strengthen the point you were trying to make.

■ **Whit kinna wey is that tae cairry oan furnenst onybody?** What sort of behaviour is that in front of others? This is withering comment on the permissive society of the 1960s, as seen through the eyes of an older generation.

■ **National brid.** The National Loaf. The one and only type of bread available during the war. Made of barnyard sweepings and often described as "Hitler's secret weapon".

First doon-the-watter trip is a wash-oot for Bill

IT was the first Doon the Wattur sail of the season for Big Bill and Wee Frank. They were pleased with themselves as they waited near the Gourock boat train for Iris and Tessa, the young ladies they were taking on the outing.

Big Bill wore a woollen purple and orange ski cap with an outsize pom-pom. Wee Frank's headgear was similar, only it was in vivid red and green.

But their enthusiasm was not shared by Iris and Tessa when they arrived. "Aw fur peety's sake!" exclaimed Iris. "Whit the heck's thae things ye've goat stuck oan yer nappers?"

"It's a perra tea-cosies," opined Tessa.

"Whit's wrang wi' them?" asked Big Bill. "Thoosants o' fellas werr them when they're ski-in' aboot oan the mountins."

"You're nutt gaun' up nae mountins," pointed our Iris. "Take aff thae wee lassies' bunnets an' stuff them in yer poakits."

But, despite all the derisive remarks, Wee Frank and Big Bill refused to dispense with their "in" headgear.

Once on board, they all descended to the small lounge bar and Big Bill ordered refreshments.

They sat for a half-hour, then Wee Frank announced. "Ah think it's time we went up fur some fresh air."

"Nae dampt fears!" said Iris. "Tessa an' me's no' gaun' up therr tae catch wur daith o' pewmonia! Youse two kin go up oan the deck – an' order us a couple merr gin-an' limes afore yiz go."

The cronies somewhat grimly carried out this request. "A deid loss," growled Wee Frank. "We wiz mugs tae bring that perr."

But Big Bill was not listening. His ever-observant eye had lighted on two prepossessing blondes who were standing on the open deck, their long tresses flying gaily in the wind.

"Therr's the kinna burds Ah like," said the big chap admiringly. "No' feart fur a wee bit breeze." "Aye," said Wee Frank thoughtfully, and, with Big Bill following wonderingly, he sauntered slowly towards the windswept maidens.

In his customary easy style, he said, "D'ye like a wee blow?"

"Ah don't know, Ah've never met ye afore," said one of the blondes. This jolly misunderstanding served to break the ice, and soon all four were chatting animatedly together.

For over an hour, the gay badinage went on. "Aw, Ah like thae caps o' yours!" cried one of the blondes. "See's a shoat o' yours."

And she took Big Bill's cap and put it on.

"Oh, deid kinky!" squeaked her friend, appreciating Wee Frank's headgear and placing it on her fair tresses.

There was much laughter at all this when Iris and Tessa emerged from below decks, and, with frosty looks, surveyed the merry scene.

"Ah don't want to brek up nuthin'," said Iris coldly. "But ye seem tae huv furgoat that we're alang wi' youse two."

Rather sheepishly the two gents rejoined Iris and Tessa. But thereafter the outing was a somewhat bleak affair.

Back in the city, the cronies convoyed the sullen damsels to the abode of Iris, where Tessa was to spend the night.

"Well, it's been a long day," sighed Wee Frank.

"It's been like a bloomin' senchurry!" declared Tessa. "We'll no' be in YOUR cump'ny again, Ah kin tell ye THAT!"

"Aw, we done all right for cump'ny," murmured the small gent complacently. "Ah've got the blondes' phone numbers, tae."

At this romantic disclosure Iris released a shrill screech of anger, and, whipping off her shoe, aimed a blow at Wee Frank's face with the heel end.

Big Bill intervened and gave her a slap.

"By goash, a perra scruff them yins!" he growled when he had to appear in court and disburse £3.

■ **They things stuck oan yer nappers**. Placed on your heads. Napper (head) is possibly from the most obvious part of your body that takes a nap. However, straightforward etymologies and assumptions of meanings should be treated with caution. The guid Scots rarely arrives at word meanings by simple routes, which is one of the many reasons it is so fascinating. There was a short-lived 1960s fashion for exuberantly-coloured woolen ski tammies.

■ **See's a shoat o' yours**. Give me a loan of yours. Shoat/shot is a brief loan, having temporary use of a thing. Can also be "shottie", especially among young people.

■ **Perra scruff them yins**. A pair of low people. "Pair" is a noun, but perra brackets the two young ladies as a unit, denoting that each is (in Bill's considered opinion) as bad as the other. The "them yins" (those ones) might appear a needless addition, but with some stress on the "them" magnifies the insult, as it suggests "them" (they) are renowned for unimpressive behaviour.

Switched-on gents make Rita blaw a fuse

EXCITEMENT again filled the air in the Okeydokey Club. The placard outside the noted dance resort gave the reason for this. It stated – "Grand Final of Switched-On Gents Contest."

Fred and His Band of Boogie Woogie Bachles gave a particularly impressive fanfare, from their wide repertoire of fanfares, to herald the entrance of Wee Andy, M.C.

The Master of Ceremonies was obviously in the grip of strong emotions. "Ladies and gentlemens, not never in the history of the Okeydokey Club has a more importanter contest never took place than the one we are now about for to witness here."

There were oohs and aahs from the crowd at the gravity of this statement.

Wee Andy went on. "The objic' is to find the most bestest-dressed gent in the area. The six finalists is noted for being what we terminate "switched-on" in their saritoral taste."

"It wid be merr tae ma taste if you wiz switched aff," came the voice of Rita the Critic.

Wee Andy directed a stern look at her. "Madam," he said, "this is neether the time and place for you, again, nor nobody else to again make remarks of no such unseemly nature."

There was some activity on the band platform as five rather unkempt figures with guitars and drums took up position.

"And here, to play throughout the contest, is a new group which I have just went and discovered," said Wee Andy. "Allow me to introduce to youse – The Nyucks!

"As each entrant parades individualistically the Nyucks, with unsingular appropriation, will give us the number, Desicatit Follower of Fashion."

A raucous sound rose from the group, only vaguely reminiscent of the original tune, and the first contestant strolled into view and stood while the Master of Ceremonies, consulting a sheet of paper, described his attire.

"Craig is wearing a primrose-coloured D.B. jacket with his green trousers," he declared. "The blue shirt and cherry-red knitted tie completes his enn sembully."

"Oh, is zat no' pathetic!" cried Rita. "If it wizny fur his face he could be mistook fur a lassie. But nae lassie could be as ugly as ZAT!"

The second contestant, a willowy youth with shoulder-length hair, made his appearance.

"Bob here bought his flowery shirt and blue velvet trousers down in London," Wee Andy announced. "No doubt youse have never saw a more striking-er outfit."

It was too much for Rita. "Ah've never saw a merr stupiter-lookin' mug in ma life!" she called.

One of the young ladies present, Noreen, took umbrage.

"That happens tae be ma boy friend!" she cried.

"Merr liker somebody's girl friend," retorted Rita. "Tell him tae gi'e his Maw back hur blouse."

"Whit! Ah'm gonny belt the gub aff that impiddint midden!" screeched Noreen, rushing over to confront Rita.

Wee Andy was quickly on the scene. "Ladies" he appealed, "kindly refrain from indulging in no unladylike conduc'!"

"Staun' back, Hauf Pint!" ordered Rita as, countering a blow from Noreen, she shot out her fist.

With his usual consummate skill, Wee Andy stepped back in the nick of time. Almost simultaneously, he emitted the famed low emergency whistle that brought his henchmen to the scene.

Rita was quickly escorted from the establishment and handed into the custody of the police.

"That pale-faced scunner wi' the knobbly knees wiz gonny hit me. Yiz aw saw it," she told the magistrate.

He shook his head sadly, and uttered just two words – "Five pounds."

■ **Rita The Critic**. The more discerning reader might be wondering why Rita is ever allowed anywhere near the Okeydokey Club. She is regularly ejected for her violent interventions. But Rita stands, of course, as representative of the straight-talking, no-airs, even fewer graces, Glesca woman. She says what she thinks and is always prepared to back up her opinions with her fists if called upon. She is, in her feisty, fisty, and sharp-tongued ways, a distillation of Glesca womanhood and, in some ways, might be regarded as an icon of feminism. Her methods may be questionable, but her attitudes could be regarded as decades ahead of their time. No one, not one person on the entire planet, could regard Rita The Critic (and those of her like who inhabited Glasgow's streets) as anything other than a force to be reckoned with.

■ **Desicatit Follower of Fashion.** Dedicated Follower Of Fashion. An approximation of the title of a 1965 hit for popular beat combo The Kinks.

Harry's pools win brings domestic strife

BIG Kate was greatly impressed by a television play that she had seen.

"This play wiz aboot a Glesca family that came inty a loat o' money," she related to her husband, Wee Dan. "An' it brung them nuthin' but trouble."

"Naw, they musta been a right buncha mugs!" scoffed the small gent. "Ah know whit AH wid dae if Ah came inty a foartune."

"Whit wid you dae?" asked his wife.

"Well, first of a' Ah'd go doon tae the licensed grocer's an' order up a case o' whisky," revealed Wee Dan. "Then Ah'd invite ma pals up fur a cellybration."

"That's the very thing the man that goat the money done in the play!" said Big Kate. "An' him an' his sons a' goat stocious an' the hale faimly wiz that unhappy."

"Aw but that wiz jist in a play oan the tillyvision," pointed out Wee Dan. "Ah've nae sons tae ladle oot booze tae. Ah'd jist huv some nice wee pairties wi' some o' ma pals, an' yer feyther wid be comin' up fur an odd hauf oot ma big coacktail cabinet."

At this juncture, and by quite a coincidence, Auld Harry, Kate's sprightly father, arrived with tumultuous news.

"Hey," he cried to his son-in-law, "ye'll never guess whit happen't tae me. Ah've gone and hud a three-poun' divi aff a' ra pools!"

"Well, ye'll be able tae buy yersel' that perra shoes ye're badly in need o'," his daughter told him.

"That's whit YOU think!" laughed the elderly gent. "Ah'd a merr pleasanter thing tae spend it oan.

"Ah've brung ye a hauf, lad. You've bought me plenty, so it's time Ah stood ma haun' in return."

To Wee Dan, this was welcome news indeed.

And before his son-in-law's fascinated gaze Auld Harry produced a bottle of whisky from his coat pocket.

Then he uttered that phrase heard with pleasure at so many social occasions in Glasgow "Getra glesses oot!"

"Ya wicked aul' spen'thrift, ye!" cried Big Kate angrily. "That's jist whit him an' me wiz talkin' aboot – folk comin' inty money an' boozin' it a' away!"

"Ach, whit's two or three poun'?" asked Auld Harry. "Let's a' huv a guid snifter!"

"Nane fur me!" cried Big Kate as her father started pouring. "Ah'm no' encouragin' yer rotten extravagance. Ye'd rather huv whisky than shoes oan yer feet."

"It's MA boattle," pointed out Auld Harry. "Ah kin dae whit Ah like wi' it!"

"Pit that boattle away this minit!" commanded the large lady. "Ye're a disgraceful aul' scunner, that's whit ye ur!"

"Oh, that's a terrible way tae talk tae yer feyther!" protested Wee Dan.

"Ah'll shut your geggie fur ye!" bellowed Big Kate. She fulfilled this sinister prognostication by giving her husband what was later technically described by Auld Harry as "an awfy hard bat oan the mooth."

A somewhat lengthy rumpus followed and was only ended when neighbours called in the police.

Big Kate was charged with breach of the peace and assault.

"Oh, whit a scannal!" she wailed in court. "Ah've never hud the polis at ma door afore!"

She was greatly relieved when, after giving her a sharp telling-off, the magistrate told her to go.

■ **Stocious**. Expressive Glasgow, and Scotland-wide, slang for drunk. Very drunk.

■ **Folk comin' inty money**. People coming in to money. The level of poverty that existed in the earlier parts of the 20th Century is almost unimaginable in the Britain of today. Existence was often hand-to-mouth. Families would spend days without food on the table. An unexpected £3 dividend from the football pools was rare and could indeed be the difference between having shoes to wear, or going around with leaky worn-through soles for a winter or even years.

■ **Scannal**. Scandal. Though interaction with the police was commonplace for some members of the working class, the better sort of household would be hugely embarrassed to "huv the polis at the door" because they saw themselves as "respectable-like".

■ **Geggie**. Expressive Glasgow slang for mouth.

Big Maisie lays a high-class youth low

ALICE was enthusing to her mother, Big Maisie, about the new boy friend, Alan, who was to call that evening and take her out for dinner.

"He reminds me o' James Bond," said the young lady. "Ye want tae see his suit, weel cut, an' the jaickit huz a rid satin linin', tae!"

"Does that make him like James Boand?" asked Big Maisie with just a soupcon of scepticism.

"Aw it's no' only that!" her daughter assured her. "Alan talks kinna like James Bond, tae. A' jerky like, an' he's sophistycatit. Knows a' about dinin' oot, an' how tae oarder waiters aboot an' aw that.

"He sounds a right nice fella," muttered her mother. She didn't have long to wait before the 007-like young gent arrived.

"How d'yew dew," he murmured suavely as Alice introduced him to her mother.

Big Maisie noted the white nylon shirt, the gaily-toned lining of the jacket, and his mysterious-looking Continental sunglasses.

"Howzit gaun?" she asked him. "Er – splendid," he replied in his laconic Bond-like way.

"Care for a cigarette?" And he offered his elegant pigskin cigarette-case to the ladies.

Quickly, he lit their cigarettes with his equally elegant lighter.

"Oh – oh, inna name o' hivvin'!" Big Maisie choked as she inhaled. "Whit's that? Oh, Ah've jist aboot burnt the gullet aff masel'!"

"Alan doesn't smoke nothin' but French cigarettes," stated Alice proudly.

"Well whit's he pit in them?" panted Big Maisie. "French beans?"

"Not exactly," said the suave young gent. And he turned to Alice. "Actually, I've ordered French beans with the dinner tonight, to go with the Supremes de Volaille," he told her.

"Oh, here, Ah've goat French beans in the gairdin therr!" said Big Maisie. "Bags o' them. Come oan an' Ah'll show ye them."

"Oh, err, thenk yew," murmured the somewhat nonplussed Alan, following her to the door and out into the back garden.

"Erreyar owererr," the large lady said proudly.

But the Bond-like gent never saw the French beans. Hampered, perhaps, by his dark glasses, he tripped over a hoe that had been strategically discarded and took what is known as "a heider" into an extremely muddy patch of ground.

There was a brief silence as Alan, his face and shirt-front plastered with mud, rose to his feet.

Big Maisie tried hard to control her mirth. She really did try. But it was impossible. The evening air reverberated with her hearty haw-haw-haws.

Alan's Bond-like suave demeanour deserted him faster than an Aston Martin DB5 can fire its hidden-behind-the-number-plate machine guns.

"Ye stupid-lookin' big midden, ye!" he yelled. "Whit ur ye laughin' at? Ah'll put a stoap tae yer cacklin'!"

He scrambled out of the mud.

However, possibly again thanks to the dark glasses, he didn't perceive that Big Maisie had picked up the hoe – until she bounced the handle smartly off his cranium.

A little later, Big Maisie learned she would have to appear in court next morning for assault and breach of the peace.

But she was quite impenitent when she faced the magistrate. "Ah gi'ed the rotten nyuck whit he deserved!" she declared.

She smiled contentedly as she paid her £3 fine.

■ **Rid satin linin'.** Red satin lining. Never trust a man with red satin lining to his suit. All working-class women should already know this.

■ **How d'yew dew.** How do you do. An affected accent gives a further clue that Alan might be a bad 'un.

■ **Volaille.** Seemingly, this is French for "poultry". The further south from Glasgow an accent is from, the more questions must be asked of the speaker's character. Anglish, with its pale, inexpressive words and accents, is bad enough, but anyone who can't say "chicken" when they mean "chicken" is obviously a daftie. They clearly canna speak nane in France. A belt on the heid with a hoe handle is the least such a person deserves.

■ **Erreyar owererr.** There they are over there. One of the greatest phrases in this book. Erreyar owererr, with its simultaneous consonant economy and ease of pronunciation, proves how a few gloriously expressive – but simple – Glaswegian words can add flavour and personality to anyone's speech. Non-Glesca folk across the world are jealous of the linguistic clarity of phrases like erreyar owererr.

Bill's comedy turn takes the life and soul oot a pairty

WEE Frank's mind was far away; even far away from the glass that stood empty before him on the bar counter.

"Whit's up wi' you the night?" asked his crony, Big Bill. "Ye're away in a dream or somethin'. Ye didny even hear me askin' ye if ye waantit anither hauf!"

"Oh, aye, sure, sure!" said the small gent with alacrity. "Ah've jist been staunnin' here thinkin'."

"Aw, don't tell me ye're still worryin' aboot that wee blonde that gi'ed ye the brush-aff at the dancin' the other night," Big Bill sighed.

"Naw, NAW, Ah'm no' thinkin' o' nae blonde!" said Wee Frank impatiently. "It's the pairty we're gaun' tae at Big Mavis's oan Setterday night. Ah think we should gi'e the cump'ny a turn."

"How d'ye mean, a turn?" asked the big chap.

"Well, ye know how the burds is aye that impressed wi' coamics," said the small chap. "They go crazy fur thon fellas Peter Cooke an' Dudley Moore. Well, Ah thought we might dae a kinna crosstalk act like them at the pairty.

"You say tae me 'I went up to Big Millie's hoose yesterday, an' she opened the front door in her nightgoon.' An' Ah say, 'That's a queer like place tae huv a front door'."

Big Bill was perplexed. "What's funny aboot THAT?" he asked. "It IS a queer place tae huv a front door."

Carefully the small chap explained the gem of wit.

They went on to further impromptu rehearsals. Wee Frank told his partner, "Nixt, Ah tell ye, 'I asked Big Millie if her grannie was in.' She said 'Naw, she's at Arbroath.' An' Ah sayed 'Okay, I'll wait till she's feenished'."

"Okay," said Big Bill, "Go on."

"That's IT!" Wee Frank told him. "Big Millie means thut her grannie as AT ARBROATH, no' AT HUR BROATH. D'ye gerrit noo?"

"Aye, Ah've goat it – but Ah'm no' sure if Ah waant it," Bill muttered. "Whit's nixt?"

"Well it's YOUR turn tae crack a gag noo," his partner informed him. "Ah tell you that Big Millie's financy deceived hur. Didny tell hur he had a widden leg. An' YOU say, 'Did she break it aff?'"

Eventually, after some trouble, the comedy double act was ready, and the night of the cronies' debut arrived.

The hostess, Big Mavis, announced to her guests – "A perra coamics is gonny gi'e yiz a turn."

The cronies, each wearing a large tartan cap to signify he was a Scots comedian, appeared.

"I went up to Big Millie's hoose last night and she opened the front door in her nightgoon," said Wee Frank. Big Bill hesitated briefly. "Wiz she at Arbroath?" he countered.

"Naw, naw, she opened the front door in her nightgoon!" his partner said desperately.

"That was a queer-like place tae have hur broath," Big Bill replied.

And before his partner could deal with this, he went on, "Big Millie broke the widden leg aff hur financy."

The audience looked on in glum silence.

Then the shrill voice of Wee Grace ended the comic turn. "Aw gi'e it up!" she yelled. "The only funny thing about youse is yer stupit-lookin' faces."

"Well, naebuddy kin ca' YOUR face funny," riposted Wee Frank. "It's tragic."

Wee Grace's gentleman friend rushed over to avenge this insult. Big Bill's fist shot out, and the gent measured his length on the floor.

Next day the big chap was in court on an assault charge.

"A deid loss," he growled as he stumped up a £5 fine. "An' Ah peyed sivvin-an'-a-tanner fur that tartan bunnet, tae."

■ **A turn**. It used to be a social norm that everyone could "do a turn" at a party, if called upon. Although Bill and Frank's Cook-Moore inspired double act, with its quickfire repartee, is a more ambitious undertaking than the more usual type of turn, a rendition of *The Old Rugged Cross*.

■ **Deid loss**. Dead loss. A sharp insult to be directed at a "turn". Mostly, a turn was enthusiastically applauded (or at least quietly tolerated) even if of not the highest quality. A deid loss is a complete failure.

■ **Financy**. Fiance.

■ **Arbroath**. A fabled and exotic holiday resort on the east coast of Scotland, breathed upon by the gentle zephyrs from the North Sea. All the delights of the western world could be had in this pleasure playground, most notably the "haddie" (locally caught and smoked haddock).

Holiday memories get Hilda a' het up

HILDA was recounting her holiday experiences to a select group of guests in her abode.

"Aw, ye canny whack Majorica fur a hoaliday. It was brawlike!" she enthused.

"Aye, it wiz a' right, Ah 'spose" commented her husband, Wee Boab, with considerably less enthusiasm. "But Ah found it too bloomin' hoat."

"Ma man wiz jist the same way when we went to Torremawhiddyecryit, in Spain," revealed Wee Madge. "Ah could hardly get him oot his scratcher – an' the sun shinin' luvly outside tae."

"If ye ask me onythin'," said Hilda with a sour glance at her spouse, "men's jist a pest when ye go oan yer hoalidays. Nivvir stoap moanin'. They should a' stey at hame an' let the weemin go by thursels."

"Ah didny huv a daicint hauf a' the time Ah wiz away!" declared the diminutive gent.

"That's a lie," Hilda countered. "It wizny the sun that made yer face rid every night. Even in the plane comin' hame ye hud a guid bucket in ye."

"Aw Ah jist had a snifter or two tae settle ma stummick," protested Wee Boab.

"Aye, lissin tae THAT lie, if ye wid!" exclaimed Hilda. "He hud the jitters because he wiz in a plane. An' when it hut a wee air poackit an' it gi'ed a wee bit of a bump aboot, he wiz scerred oot his wits."

"Ah wiz nut!" cried Wee Boab.

"Ye wiz sutt!" said his wife. "Ye went inty the hold-all while Ah wiz busy readin' ma magazine an' took the boattle o' brandy Ah wiz bringin' hame fur ma maw.

"An' then when Ah went tae declerr it tae the Customs Ah fun thur wiz hee-haw left in't."

"Naw, naw. The brandy was medizzynal. A' doctors will tell ye that. It was jist tae keep me fae bein' air sick," Wee Boab assured her.

"Well Ah wiz fair sick o' you by the time we goat hame," Hilda assured him. "An' Ah hud tae kick ye three times oan the shin tae get ye tae stoap singin' yer party piece *Granny's Hieland Hame* in the airport bus."

"Ach we wiz better at Dunoon," said her husband. "A' that sun jist made you crabbit, an' ye ett that much ye burst the zipp aff yer new froack.

"Then thur wiz the time ye ett the fried oactypus and wiz moanin' a' night wi' the pain in yer peeny."

"Aye, an' when Ah asked you tae gi'e me a pouther in a glass of watter, ye gi'ed me wan in a gless o' yer chape shirry-wine," Hilda reminded him.

"Near gi'ed me the bile!"

"Well, it shut ye up fur a bit, onywey," commented Wee Boab.

The remark angered the lady. "Ah'll shut YOU up – right noo," she bellowed.

Before the rest of the company could intervene, she bounced her fist off her husband's forehead.

A struggle ensued, and the police were called.

In court on a breach charge, Hilda disclosed, "Ma man sayed somethin' that made me loss ma temper a' sudden-like."

The magistrate shook his head, gave her a severe ticking-off, and told her to go.

■ **Brawlike**. Braw is good, fine, splendid, excellent. The addition of the "like" is an intensifier even to this most fulsome praise. Braw probably originated in the lowlands or Borderlands, hence Galashiels' Braw Lad competitions (a sort of beauty pageant for galumphin' big laddies), but has spread throughout Scotland.

■ **Peeny**. A word for the stomach or stomach area. The Anglish corrupted word "pinafore" is probably derived from this.

■ **Pouther**. A powder. Headache or gastric remedies were often purchased in powdered form, individually wrapped. Pills are now more common.

■ **Ah fun thur wiz hee-haw in't**. Rather to my surprise, I found that there was nothing left in the bottle.

■ **Dunoon**. A sort of west-coast version of Arbroath, if possible even more grim. And without the haddies. However, the open-air swimming pool was rumoured to be almost a degree warmer, on average. It was still freezin' though!

Missing her beauty sleep made Isa an ugly customer

ISA appeared to be even more disgruntled than usual as she prepared to retire for the night. "Ah'll be wide awake fur oors," she informed her husband, Jim. "Ah don't know whit's gi'en me this bloomin' insoamnia."

"Aw, don't worry," he retorted, not looking up from the racing form guide in the paper. "A guid night's sleep'll soon cure yer insoamnia."

His wife gave him a short, bleak look. "Ya stupit ass!" she growled.

Jim, as was his habit, was asleep almost as soon as his head touched the pillow. But, as she had predicted, Isa lay awake long after midnight.

But eventually, she sank into fitful slumber.

Suddenly she was wide awake. She sat up and looked at the alarm clock on the bedside table.

It indicated 2.15am.

If it hadn't been the alarm that woke her, then she fell to wondering what it might have been? Then the sound of a shrill giggle came from the street. It was followed by a high-pitched female cry, "Ye're an awfy man, Fraser!"

An angry imprecation escaped Isa when she recognised the voice of Carole, the young lady who resided in the bottom flat of the tenement.

Isa rose from her pit and crossed to the window.

Looking balefully down, she saw Carole and her long-haired cavalier, Fraser.

He was giving vent to another of his cutting witticisms, and once again Carole's shrill giggle cleft the silence of the night.

Isa threw up the window and leaned out. "Hey, youse!" she called. "Ur yiz awerr that it's quarter pas' two in the moarnin'?"

Fraser looked up. Witty as ever, he called back, "Thanks fur tellin' us. Ah'll pit ma watch right."

Again, Carole giggled maniacally. And once more she informed the young gent, "Oh, ye're an awfy man, Fraser!"

"D'ye cry that oabjic' a MAN?" exclaimed Isa scornfully. "His herr's longer than yours! Ye widny huv catched ME gaun' aboot wi' a thing like that when AH wiz a lassie!"

"When ye wiz a lassie naebody wid WAANT tae go aboot wi' ye, Ah'm shair," riposted Fraser. "Even thae Victorian fellas wiz a bit partic'lar aboot who they wiz saw wi'."

Carole again laughed appreciatively, and at length, over the brilliance of this sally.

"Away an' pit oan yer herr net an' get away tae yer scratcher," Isa bellowed at the long-haired young gent.

And to Carole she called, "An' you, it's time you wiz huvvin' yer beauty sleep. Ye're badly in need o' it."

"Away you an' pit in yer wallies," Fraser shouted up to the angry lady, "If ye don't watch oot some caur driver'll mistake yer mooth fur the entrance tae the Clyde Tunnel."

This adjuration sent Carole into yet more peals of laughter, perhaps with a somewhat provocative ring to them.

Her champion turned to her with satisfaction. "That'll learn hur tae stoap flingin' cracks at us!" he guffawed.

However, as his back was to the window he didn't observe that the infuriated Isa had flung something else.

A large scrubbing brush flew through the air and hit the young gent on the back of the head.

After this artillery attack, further tumultuous scenes, and exchanges of views, ensued.

On the arrival of the police, Isa was charged with assault and breach of the peace.

"It's a cryin' disgrace that a daicint wumman huz tae end up in coort over a perra long-herred numbskulls!" she declared to the magistrate.

He let her off with fines amounting to £5.

■ **His herr's longer than yours!** The longer hairstyles that appeared in the 1960s were regarded with great disdain by the older generation. Men who had been called up to the forces during the war, or had tholed their two years of National Service, were given short back and sides, and many of them carried this into civilian life. This was the mark of a man, and their womanfolk agreed. Long hair was a sign of decadence, frivilousness . . . and darker suspicions.

■ **That oabjic'.** That object. When you aren't even afforded a name, the opinion of the speaker is clear.

■ **The entrance tae the Clyde Tunnel.** A gaping black hole. Being compared to a four-lane connection between Whiteinch and Govan should not be seen as praise.

Toothache make's Willie's dream date a nightmare

ON the eve of his big date with Dawn, Willie had his long hair shampooed and set.

He ensured that his Carnaby Street-style suit, the shirt with the frilly front, and his light suede chukka boots were all in perfect order.

But early next morning Willie awoke to discover that fate had dealt him a cruel blow.

He had developed a raging toothache.

At breakfast, his younger brother greeted him with a disconcerting observation. "Here Willie, yer ja's no' hauf swole!" he said. "Ye'll no' be able tae keep yer date wi' the Dawn burd!"

"Aah'm keepin' that date, nae matter whut," said the lovestruck one grimly, surveying the ham and eggs that he was quite unable to eat.

Later that evening, attired in his best, he was on his way to meet the prepossessing damsel.

If he thought that the sight of her would banish the pain in his aching jaw he was sadly mistaken.

Dawn's first words when they met were, "Oh, help, yer face is up like a bloon!"

"Aye. Ah've goat toothache," exclaimed Willie.

"Oh, zat whit it is?" said the glamorous maiden. "Ah wiz wunnerin' if Ah hud made a mistake an' hudny noticed ye'd a great big bawface!"

She laughed merrily at the thought. Willie found himself a little disappointed at her lack of sympathy.

"It's a big yin," he said.

"Yer face or the tooth?" queried Dawn. And once again her merry laughter rang out.

"Ye never laugh at onybody wi' a sprain't ankle," she went on. "But ye aye laugh at somebody wi' a swallt face. It's funny how ye dae that, intit?"

"Hangava funny," growled the sufferer, rapidly becoming further disillusioned. "Wherr d'ye want tae go?"

"The dancin', of course!" said Dawn. "Ah aye get ma Friday date tae lumber me tae the dancin'!"

"Let's go tae the dancin'," sighed Willie.

Soon they were in a nearby dance hall, contorting their frames and heads, as modern standards of dancing dictate, to the music of an over-amplified group.

But every thumping beat seemed to go through Willie like a blow directly on his tooth.

He closed his eyes, and toyed with the idea of rushing from the dance hall and making for home.

Suddenly he became aware of a sound that was even more strident than that of the beat group. Dawn was laughing again, this time at full volume.

"Aw, here, ye want tae see yersel'!" she choked.

"Whidd'ye mean?" asked Willie, glowering at her.

"Ye look that funny wi' yer eyes shut an' yer big jaw bobbin' up an' doon therr!" she shrieked.

It was the end of the date.

Her face received a resounding slap and Willie headed for the exit.

But there was no escape. He was promptly handed over to the police and charged with assault.

His swelling had disappeared by the time the case called at court.

"Ah'm well red o' thon moanster," he growled when he was fined £6. And he wasn't referring to his now-extracted tooth.

■ **No hauf swole… Up like a bloon… Big jaw bobbin' up an' doon**. Various terms for degrees of facial swelling, a scale not universally followed by the medical profession.

■ **Bawface**. Sometimes bawheid. Face like a football. An insult, but one which, as Dawn points out, would often evoke humour.

■ **Hangava**. Very.

■ **A resounding slap.** These were more violent times, even with a thumpin' toothache and an unsympathetic lumber, it says little for Willie that he resorted to violence. However, throughout these pages, violence is dealt with by the law. No aggressor gets off with dealing out slaps, dunts or whacks. Even in times of vastly different standards of behaviour, violence rarely went unpunished. Every one of the stories in this book serves as a warning against taking the law into one's own hands, or fists.

Millie's vigorous Cha-cha-cha is too much for Wee Andy M.C.

IT was Grand Cha-Cha-Cha Night at the Okeydokey Club. Eagerly the patrons thronged round the band platform to await the appearance of Wee Andy, M.C.

But suddenly, in place of the usual fanfare, came the slow rhythmic rattle and jangle of Latin-American percussion instruments. Then Fred and his Band of Boogie-Woogie Bachles got to their feet and chanted – "Cha-Cha-Cha."

With a stirring, if somewhat shrill, cry of "Ole!" the Master of Ceremonies made his entrance.

"Ladies and gents, tonight I wish for to introduce to youse the latest dance – the Cha-Cha-Cha!" he announced.

"Not only that, but we are going to learn youse how for to be expert Cha-Cha-Cha-ers!"

"Oh, Ah waant tae dae ra Cha-Cha-Cha!" cried Big Millie, carried away by enthusiasm.

"Certingly," said Wee Andy. "But, firstly, permit me for to explain what is going to be did. We are going for to be showed the steps by two unimitible exponuents.

"Ladies and gents, the Emperor and Empress of Cha-Cha-Cha!" Once again, the orchestra struck up their slow Latin-American rhythm.

The Emperor and Empress, a diminutive, serious-faced couple in Spanish attire, performed a somewhat sinuous, if disjointed, dance.

"Oh, Ah could dae that!" cried Big Millie excitedly.

"Kindly do not make no comments while the dancers is dancing," requested Wee Andy. "Just be good enough for to observe the rowtine."

The Emperor and Empress finished their demonstration and received an enthusiastic ovation.

Then the Master of Ceremonies held up a hand to still the applause. "Now, youse have all saw how the Cha-Cha-Cha is did," he said. "Next, I am going for to request youse to please take your partners and try for to emuliate the experts! Ole!"

Yet again, the slow rhythm began, and soon the dance floor was filled.

But Big Millie could not find a partner.

Then she saw the Emperor of Cha-Cha-Cha himself as he

inspected the dancers. "Here, Ah'll dae it wi' YOU!" she cried, advancing on the diminutive expert in the Spanish costume.

He gaped at her apprehensively. "Aw, kin ye no' talk Inglish?" said the large girl pityingly. "Och, it dizny matter. Come oan!" And grabbing him with both hands, she almost carried him to the dance floor.

"Hey, whitsa gemme? Whitsa gemme?" cried the artiste when he found his breath. "Ah don't want tae dance!"

Big Millie staggered back, startled. "Oh, jings, ye're no' a furriner at a'!" she exclaimed.

"Naw, Ah'm no'!" retorted the "Emperor" resentfully. "An' lay me alane!"

Wee Andy then approached. "Come now," he said tactfully to Big Millie, "I am afraid the artistes is not permitted for to dance with the patrons. You see –"

"Never mind rat!" cried the large girl. "The Cha-Cha-Cha'll be feenished afore we get stertit! Come oan! You an' me'll huv a go at it!" So saying, she took hold of the Master of Ceremonies and embarked on her own rather exaggerated version of the new dance.

Wee Andy struggled free from her bear-like grip.

"Madam," he said, with dignity, "allow me for to inform you that the Manidgemint does not dance."

"Ach away or Ah'll skite the skull aff ye!" exclaimed Big Millie in a burst of exasperation. Then, swinging a large fist, she endeavoured to carry out her decapitation threat.

With his customary adroitness, the Master of Ceremonies avoided the blow. Simultaneously he emitted the low emergency whistle.

Later, in court on a breach of the peace charge, Millie gave a somewhat inaccurate account of the incident.

"Ah wis jist daen' ra Cha-Cha-Cha wi' him, an' ma haun' wiz wavin' in the air, like," she said, demonstrating the movement. Her fib availed her naught. She was fined £1.

■ **The Okeydokey Club**. Rita has clearly been banned from the Okeydokey Club, to no one's surprise. The enthusiastic approach of Big Millie wouldn't have suited her anyway. It isn't surprising that stories featuring characters other than Rita would be set in a social club. Such clubs, many would have been small dance halls rather than social clubs, were widespread. They sold drink and were full of Glasgow folk with all their enthusiasms and habits — they would always have been likely to feature in court stories.

Big blaw-up over women wearing trousers

ARCHIE and Davie, attired in their new charcoal grey suits, waited patiently at the street corner. "D'ye think thae judies'll turn up?" asked Archie a trifle anxiously.

His crony beat a severe look upon him. "Judies!" he echoed frostily. "That is nutt no way to talk about Shirley and Lucy. Fur once-t we've goat a date wi' a perr o' dames that's been well brung up."

"Ye're right therr," conceded Archie. "Shirley's that partic'lur aboot hur appearance tae. Thon night we took them tae the pictures, she spent hauf the time combin' her herr."

"Aw, aye. They've goat class," agreed Davie. "Thur no' like this perr that's comin' alang."

And he stared disapprovingly at two young ladies in the distance. One wore blue trousers and the other red trousers.

"If therr's wan thing Ah canny staun', it's weemin in troosers," stated Archie, averting his eyes from the grievous sight.

"Me an' a'," said Davie, turning his back on the betrousered damsels.

Two minutes later, they were greeted by that well-known Glasgow salutation – "Hullawrerr!"

The cronies turned and were dumbfounded to see that the trouser-wearers who had been approaching were none other than Shirley and Lucy.

"Oh, Ah didny … didny reckanise ye!" faltered Archie.

"We knowed ye widny!" cried Shirley, who was wearing the red trousers.

"We pit oan wur jeans because it wiz that dampt cauld. Thur rerr fur the cauld weather."

Davie, appalled, could think of only one thing – getting the young ladies out of sight as quickly as possible.

"Well, whit aboot gaun' tae the picturs acroass the street therr?" he suggested.

"Heh, Ah thought we wiz gaun' tae the dancin' the night?" said Lucy.

"The dancin'?" mumbled Archie. "But yiz canny dance in thae…"

"Canny dance in wur troosers?" exclaimed Shirley. "That's

whaur you're wrang, pal! We kin eckshully dance mair better in them. Sure we kin, Lucy?"

"Of course we kin," said Shirley briskly. "Come oan, let's get gaun'. Ah could dae wi' a spoat o' jive tae warm me up."

"Wait a minnit," said Davie desperately. "Me an' the china here's no' very hoat at the jivin'.'"

"Ach, ye don't need tae worry aboot that!" Lucy assured him. "We'll learn ye."

There was nothing for it. The cronies had to take the young ladies to the small dance hall.

Archie and Davie were greatly embarrassed by their reception. Wolf whistles resounded throughout the hall.

Then, clear above the clamour, came the somewhat strident voice of Wee Sadie. "A coupla blinkin' bachles in thur pyjamas err!" she cried.

Shirley, who was vainly trying to teach Archie the intricacies of jive, stopped between a rock and a roll. "Haw, ur you gonny let that wee midden talk tae me like that?" she indignantly asked her chap.

"She canny talk ony other way," he said. "Hur wallies don't fit hur awfy well."

Shirley gave him a keen look. "Ya scunner!" she howled. "Ye're takkin' the mickey oota me!"

Without further ado she smacked Archie's face. He then grabbed her arms to prevent a further onslaught.

Lucy wrongly assumed her girl friend was being roughly treated. She gave a yell, dashed up to Archie and pummelled him in the back with her fists. Davie, in turn, tried to pull Lucy away.

A noisy scene ensued. It culminated in the foursome being ejected. Next day Shirley and Archie appeared in court on breach of the peace charges. The young lady wept and was admonished.

Archie was morose. "Anough tae mak' ye immigrate tae St Kilda!" he growled as he paid his £1 fine.

■ **Women in trousers**. It was rarely done. Indeed, a woman going to a 1950s dance hall in trousers was a very rare sight. It was considered daring, but sometimes a little low, to show off a woman's lower curves in jeans. Hence the reported wolf-whistles. The one disapproving shout, you will note, comes from a woman, Wee Sadie.

■ **Judies**. The female equivalent of Teddy Boys in the 1950s.

■ **China**. China plate, mate.

A Carnaby Street-type comes a cropper

JANETTE and Tony were the most picturesque couple at the dancing.

The young lady was wearing a brightly-coloured trouser suit and languidly smoking a cigarette in a long holder, as was the done thing in certain fashionable London haunts . . . though fewer Glasgow dance emporiums.

Audrey Hepburn was known to smoke in a similar fashion, and would have fitted right in at the Saturday night dancin'.

For his part, Tony had on a light-blue military jacket, and red, flared trousers with a green stripe down the outside seam. His hair extended to his shoulders.

They surveyed the dancing crowd in a rather supercilious manner.

"Er a' a shower o' scruff, ur they no?" observed Janette loftily.

"So they ur," agreed Tony.

Then they were silent again for quite some time. Suddenly the young lady gave a squeak of excitement. She had noticed that the cigarette was no longer in her long holder.

"Oh, heh, wherr ma faaag?" she exclaimed.

Losing her poise entirely, she looked on and then under the table.

Stating the blatantly obvious, "It musta fell oot yer holder," opined Tony sagaciously.

"Aye, ah see that, but wherr huz it went tae?" asked Janette, mystified. "Ah turn't ma heid tae look at the group, an' when Ah tried tae draw oan ma fag, it wizny therr!"

"How d'ye mean? Izzit yer heid that wizny therr?" asked her escort, possibly an attempt at humour, possibly not.

"Naw, ma FAAAG wizny therr!" Janette informed him.

"Well, Ah've nae idea wherr it's went tae," said Tony, shrugging his epaulettes.

Two seconds later, however, he became aware of the cigarette's whereabouts.

With a cry of pain and alarm, he clapped his hands to his head and sprang to his feet. "Oh, hivvins, ye've burn't ma heid!" exclaimed the young gent.

"Ye musta goat yer napper in the wey o' ma fag when Ah turn't tae look at the group," said Janette. "That's sheer cerrlessness, ye know."

"Aw hey, it's no' ME that's cerrless!" protested Tony. "If ye waant tae smoke a fag in a holder that length ye should know how tae haun'le it."

The discussion was continuing apace when Janette and Tony noticed that they were being watched with interest by Wee Jim and his friend Dorothy.

"Hur fag fell oot her holder inty his herr!" Wee Jim informed his partner.

"Aye, they wiz sittin' therr awfy toaffy-nosed till he goat hoat-heidit!" Dorothy pointed out.

And she and her friend laughed uproariously at the bon mot.

"She near burnt the heid aff hur Carnaby Street pal," said Wee Jim. "Mind ye, he could dae wi' some o' the herr burn't aff him. Ah thought he wiz Kathy Kirby when he walked in."

Tony took exception to this and demonstrated his undoubted masculinity by giving Wee Jimmy "wan wirra heid," as a witness later described it.

The demonstration cost him £7 when he appeared in court on an assault charge.

■ **Hur Carnaby Street pal.** Her friend, affecting a Carnaby Street style of clothing. This of-its-time tale is from 1967 and reflects the cutting edge of fashion. Long hair for men was "in", as was smoking with a long holder, brightly-hued clothes and epaulette-decorated military-styled coats. The varied fashion boutiques of Carnaby Steert, London W1, were seen as the heart of these trends. However, as this tale shows, many down-to-earth citizens of Glasgow regarded these fashionistas with a critical, if not amused, eye.

■ **Ah thought he wiz Kathy Kirby**. Long hair and brightly-hued, unisex clothing notwithstanding, any suggestion that compromised a man's masculinity would not be tolerated. There was a fine line between objective fashion criticism and deadly insult.

■ **Toaffy-nosed**. Toffee-nosed. This expression has nothing to do with the sugary sweet, but refers to being (or regarding oneself as) a "toff".

■ **Wan wirra heid**. The famous "Glasgow kiss". A correctly-executed head-butt brought the butter's forehead into contact with the bridge of the buttee's nose at high velocity. A successful "wan wirra heid" was a debilitating blow to the butt receiver, in most cases signifying an end-point to hostilities.

A car and sundry luxuries cause a close-head clash

THE news swept through the street like wildfire. Carrie's husband, Jim, had purchased a car.

It wasn't a big car. Nor was it new. But its very presence outside the close leading to Carrie's abode was enough to fill the hearts of her neighbours with envy.

"Fancy hur huvvin' a caur!" exclaimed Becky to a group of ladies at the close-mouth. "Ah'd like tae know whaur hur an' hur man gets a' the cash."

"She's goat a tillyvision set an' a waashin' machine an' a'," revealed Wee Minnie. "It bates me how they dae it."

Speculations came from all sides.

"Hur man's a spiv."

"They're runnin' a shebeen."

"Hur aul' skinflint o' a mither left hur a paackit."

In the midst of all this theorising, Carrie and her husband appeared and made to enter the car.

An exclamation of surprise came from Becky. "Oh, help, she's goat a fur stole an a'," she cried.

"The green-eyed moanster's rearin' its ugly heid again," observed Carrie to her husband.

"Don't you cry me nae names, Lady Muck!" shrilled Becky. "Don't think because ye've a saickint-haundit motor caur an' a bit rabbut skin roon' yer neck that ye kin say whit ye like tae folks."

Carrie received this statement with commendable calm. "I did nutt enter into no conversation with you," she said with dignity as she settled herself into the front seat of the car.

Becky put her angry face down at the open window. "Some folks lives hangava high an' Ah'd like tae know hoo they dae it," she said.

"Some folks lives hangava low," retorted Carrie, "An' Ah KNOW hoo they dae it. They're never oota booze shoaps."

"Oh, whit a' insult, hen," said Wee Minnie sympathetically to Becky. "An' you oan the waggun fur nearly a week."

At this juncture, Big Nell arrived on the scene. "Whit's gaun oan here?" she asked the group. "Is it an accydint? Somebody hurtit?"

"Somebody's GONNY get hurtit – but it'll be nae accydint," Becky informed her.

"Stert up the caur, Jim," Carrie said to her husband. "Ah've listen't anough tae toerags fur wan day."

"Toerags!" came the indignant chorus from all the outraged ladies.

"Ah'll learn hur tae cry us that!" shouted Becky.

Her hand thereupon flashed into the car and Carrie received a stinger on the face.

The car door immediately flew open and Carrie emerged and confronted her attacker.

"See ma stole's no' stole," she said, throwing her fur to her husband. "Ah'm gonny skite the heid aff this getherup."

Big Nell stepped forward with the intention of acting the peacemaker. But she received a thump on the head that caused her to stagger back, braying loudly.

Becky took fright and ran off, screeching that well-known Glasgow S.O.S. – "Murder! Polis!"

As Big Nell found her breath and was advancing upon Carrie, the constabulary arrived.

Becky and Carrie were each booked for breach of the peace.

Counter allegations rang round the court, but the magistrate silenced the angry duo with three little words – "Two pounds each."

■ **Spiv**. UK-wide slang, popularised during World War Two, for a man who made a living dealing by disreputable deals, or buying and selling black market goods. The archetypal "spiv" dressed in flashy suits and seemed to have access to lots of money.

■ **Car. Tillyvision. Fur stole. Waashin' machine.** It's a long list of luxuries that might make any tenement-dweller suspicious. Just where DID Jim and Carrie get all that money?

■ **Getherup**. Gatherup (of strange, disparate, uncomplimentary parts). Another in the long, long list of Glasgow insults.

■ **Lady Muck**. Another insults. This barb would be reserved for people who thought themselves better than their peers, or were percieved to be thinking themselves better than their peers.

Supper date wi' twa smashers gets stormy for Bill and Frank

BIG Bill and Wee Frank had had a fairly strenuous social round. "Ah'm fagged oot wi' a' thae late oors," confessed the big chap. Ah think we should stey in the night an' get tae wur scratchers early fur a chinge."

"Naw, we canny dae THAT!" said Wee Frank. "Huv' ye furgoat we're gaun' up tae Iris's hoose fur wur supper the night?"

"Aw, hivvins, could you no' go yersel'?" sighed Big Bill. "Ah'm ferr wabbit."

"Ye'll HUV tae go," said his crony. "Iris is gonny play us hur records. An', besides, ye huvny met hur sister."

"Her sister?" repeated Big Bill with rapidly awakening interest. "Ah didny know she hud wan."

"Oh, aye – Yvonne," Wee Frank disclosed. "She's jist like Iris, a nabsaloot cracker. She's merr blonder than Iris, an' she –"

"When ur we due at thur hoose?" interrupted the big chap.

"Roon aboot eight," said Wee Frank. "It'll jist be a wee quiet night – a bite o' supper an' listenin' tae records."

That evening, at eight o'clock sharp, the cronies presented themselves at the abode of Iris.

"We'll go inty ra den," said the young lady, leading the way to a largish room. It was furnished in the contemporary manner – a divan, cocktail cabinet, record-player, and cushions, pop discs, and women's magazines tastefully scattered about.

"This is where Yvonne an' me spends wur time when," went on Iris. "Ma murra's in ra urra room wi' hur tillyvision. TV-mad, she is.

"Yvonne an' me jist looks at Top of the Pops an' Jukebox Jury, an' rat soart o' hing. We're happy when therr's a baun' gaun'."

"Is yur sister watchin' the tillyvision the noo?" asked Big Bill, disappointed at seeing no sign of the prepossessing Yvonne.

"Naw, she's oot," Iris told him. "Ye'll never guess wherr she's went! She's away up tae a wumman's hoose tae buy a carpet!"

The two gents sat on the divan and, with Iris, listened to the outpourings of the Rolling Stones, Mr P. J. Proby, the Who, The Kinks, and sundry other apostles of latter-day culture.

"Yer sister's takin' quite a while tae buy that carpet," said Wee Frank after a particularly strident spasm from the record-player.

"Aw, Ah know whit's keepin' Yvonne!" said Iris. "Ah bet ye she's went tae the chip shope fur a coupla pies fur hur supper."

"Ah'm kinna partial tae a pie masel'," murmured Wee Frank a trifle wistfully. "Sometimes Ah've wan fur ma supper."

"Oh, no' me!" Iris stated. "A' Ah huv efter six a'cloke at night is a cuppa coaffy an' a coupla sweetie biscuits – we'll huv that when Yvonne comes in."

The cronies exchanged fleeting glances of despair.

"Whit wid yiz like tae hear noo?" asked the young lady.

"The kettle singin'," muttered Big Bill. "WHO singin'?" asked Iris.

"Aye, The Who," Wee Frank said hastily. "Play that yin by the Who laddies again." And she did.

It was late in the evening when the door swung open and Yvonne made her appearance. She nodded curtly to the guests, then turned excitedly to her sister with the information, "Ah've got the carpet! Rodney's tryin' tae get it in the door."

Turning to the guests, she suggested, "You fellas gi'e him a haun'. Don't let puir Rodney dae a' ra work!"

With a certain glumness the cronies complied. Rodney, the sisters' younger brother, turned out to be a thin stripling of a lad.

"It's stuck," he said, leaning exhausted against the bulky and rather well-worn carpet.

"Ease it oot oan tae the landin' an' bring it in again," ordered Yvonne.

"It seems terrible heavy," commented Iris. "We'll never be able tae lay that carpet wursels."

"Naw, but we've three fellas here that kin dae it", announced Yvonne. "Whirraboot it, fellas? Yiz kin shift the divan an' the coacktail cabinet an' that inty the loabby. Then ye kin..."

"Nuthin' daen'," said Wee Frank. "Ma jaickit an' troosers is a' cover't wi' oose an' durt a'readies aff yer aul' carpet. Ah'm fur aff."

"Oh, ya ignurint little pup ye!" screeched Yvonne. And she darted forward with fist upraised.

Big Bill caused her to desist by the simple method of placing his hand over her face and pushing her down upon the divan.

"A deid loss," he said later, when he appeared in court on an assault charge and was fined £6. "We never even goat that cuppa coaffy an' the two wee sweetie biscuits!"

■ **Ah'm ferr wabbit.** I am quite exhausted. The heavily-pronounced final T gives a vehemence to the word that strengthens the meaning considerably.

■ **A baun' gaun'.** A band going. The sound of a musical group. Trendy lassies of all eras would say the same.

■ **Oose an' durt.** Woolen fluff and dirt.

Rita's considered opinion of jazz music

THE notice outside the Okeydokey Club declared: "Tonight: Very Special Celebrity Guest Artiste."

An excited buzz swept the young ladies and gentlemen. Rumours flew that the guest might be Tommy Steele.

Then, from Fred and his Band of Boogie-Woogie Bachles, came a particularly impressive fanfare. Wee Andy M.C. made his grand entrance. "Ladies and gents," he said solemnly. "I am proud for to inform youse that our star guest tonight is a gentleman who youse have all been waiting to hear from."

"Oh, goash, it IS Tammy!" came a tense interjection.

Wee Andy ignored this. "At considerable expense," he went on, "We have brung along one of the stars of the modern jazz group that has did so well at the Burgh Hall.

"We have none urrer than that virtuosity of the electrical dulcimore, Mr Chico McWhirter!"

With these words, and amid a dull groan of disappointment, the Master of Ceremonies pulled away a white sheet to reveal, on the band platform, a vibraphone. Simultaneously Mr Chico McWhirter made his appearance.

A gasp of surprise went up when it was seen that the virtuoso was attired in morning dress. The air was filled with such speculations as – "He's just came fae a waddin'!" and "Whit's this wur gettin' noo?"

Wee Andy raised a hand for silence.

"Well, now, Mr McWhirter," he said genially. "What are you going fur to render us upon your electrical dulcimore?"

"Well, I would like furty play yiz a number entitled 'Variations on a theme from Nellie Dean' which I have wrote myself," said Chico. "Me and the boys featured it in our own show, 'Jazz at ra Barra'!"

"Splendid!" exclaimed Wee Andy.

Chico turned and regarded the rhythm section of the Boogie Woogie Bachles. They regarded him right back.

"Wan-two-'hree-four!" cried Chico. And with that he assailed his instrument with great gusto.

The audience watched stolidly as a mixture of sounds that didn't quite add up to a tune were attempted by Chico.

Suddenly the virtuoso stopped playing, threw back his head and uttered a strange unworldly cry – "Ooolyakoo!"

This utterance was clearly designed to throw the jazz addicts present into a frenzy.

Instead, there was gloomy silence from the audience. Then it was broken by a scornful female cry – "Away ya mug ye!"

Wee Andy directed a warning glare at Rita the Critic, for it had been her cry, who was standing close to the vibraphone.

Chico played on. But, during his next break, he addressed himself to the close-by Rita in an American accent strongly reminiscent of the Galllowgate. "Ah reckon you don't dig ma kinda music, babe," he said.

"Ah'd like tae dig a ruddy hole an' shove you an' yer bloomin' electrical dulcymoor inty it!" retorted Rita.

The virtuoso resumed his playing.

"Ye kin play hee-haw, Mac!" the young lady shouted up at him. Thereupon Chico leaned forward and played a short but intriguing cadenza on Rita's coiffure.

Recognising a sign of forthcoming apocalypse when he saw one, Wee Andy strode forward. "Now, now, kindly do not let us have no disagreeableness," he said. "And may I say that artistes is nutt permitted for to play upon the craniums of patrons."

"Well, she gi'es me the jandies," explained Chico.

"Dae Ah?" said Rita, who had displayed remarkable restraint up to that point.

She grabbed the side of the vibraphone and sent it and its player crashing to the floor in a jumbled jangling heap.

"This is the most monstrousest thing I have ever saw!" exclaimed Wee Andy. Without hesitation he emitted the low emergency whistle.

Rita and the virtuoso were summarily escorted from the premises. They glared at each other with deep hatred when they appeared in court next day and stumped up 30s each.

■ **Jazz**. Only a true optimist would have attempted to introduce experimental jazz to the patrons of the Okeydokey Club.

■ **A short but intriguing cadenza**. Only a true fool would be such a bad judge of character as to provoke a Glasgow woman of the likes of Rita. She let him off surprisingly lightly.

■ **Away ya mug ye**. The "away" means so more than merely "go away". Though the meaning of "ya mug ye" cannot be taken as anything other than highly uncomplimentary. There is a world of disrespect, dismissiveness and displeasure within the phrase.

Eddie the poet's sweet talk brings sour comments

EDDIE, wrapped in gloom, was seated by the fire when his friends, Roy and Wee Boab, dropped in to inquire if he would accompany them to their usual hostelry.

"Uch, naw,"he said. "Go yersels. Ah widny be very good cump'ny. Tae tell ye the truth, Ah jist waant tae be alone."

"Aw, hivvins, it's two nights since ye hud a hauf!" exclaimed Roy. "Ye canny go on like this. We've a' hud disappointmints. Ye waant tae furget aboot that burd."

Eddie rose and stared at him, aghast. "Whit ur ye sayin'?" he cried. "How can Ah furget aboot Nicky? Ye canny turn yer emotions aff like a tap, ye know."

"Ye'll HUV tae," stated Wee Boab. "The Nicky dame huzz made it plain she dizny fancy ye. Snap oota it. Thur bags o' urra burds."

"Ah don't waant nae urra burd!" declared the lovestruck one dramatically. "Nicky's the only wan Ah fancy. Oh, if Ah could only get hur tae go oot wi' me wanst!"

His friends were concerned about him. They sat pondering the problem gravely. After much thought, Roy opined, "Ah think a hauf or two an' a coupla pints o' heavy wid help ye."

Eddie shook his head sadly. "Naw, naw, that would only make me merr worser," he said. "This is a thing Ah've goat tae work oot fur masel' – whether Ah kin face life wi'oot hur, or immigrate tae Canada or someplace."

"Immygrate! Jist because a burd'll no' –" began Roy. Wee Boab gesticulated to him to be silent.

"Ah've goat an idea!" he said. "Ye know how Nicky likes po'try an' wiz hingin' aboot wi' a fella that ackchally writ some pomes?"

Eddie nodded, his expression even more anguished. "Aw, she tell't me aboot him," he muttered. "Wee pale face fella. She wiz a' excited because he got a pome printit in some magazine or urrer."

"Aye, well listen," went on Wee Boab. "Why don't YOU write a pome aboot Nicky an' send it tae hur? Burds is romantic, ye know. They go fur that kinna stuff."

"D'ye think SHE would?" asked Eddie. "If Ah thought it wid… Ach, but Ah couldny mak up a pome!"

"We'll a' huv a go at it," said Wee Boab. "Roy here's no' a bad haun' at the rhymin'. D'ye mind the leatherin' ye goat fur thon pome ye writ oan the school wa'?"

"Aye," said Roy. "Get oot the pincils an' bits o' paper an' we'll huv a bash at it. Eftir a', in the auld days fellas writ pomes tae weemin. Burns even writ 'Tae a Moose'."

"Did he get a reply?" asked Wee Boab.

Eventually, after much pencil-chewing and anguish, the poem was finished. "That should dae the trick," Wee Boab told Eddie. "Read it oot till we hear how it sounds."

The manuscript trembled in the hands of the spurned swain as he started to intone the imperishable words:

When first I met you, Nick-eh, my dear,
Love filled ma hert, that is quite clear,
Your beauty sweeped me aff my feet,
I see in dreams your face so sweet.
My love for you will e'er be great.
Please favour me with just wan date.

He was shocked to hear the sounds of shrill female laughter. In the doorway stood his sister, Carole, and her friend, Tessa.

"Whit ur yiz laughin' at?" asked Eddie angrily.

"You staunnin' therr spoutin' a loada rubbidge," Carole explained.

"'I see in dreams your face so sweet'," Tessa quoted at him. Then she asked, "Don't tell me that refers tae that daffy Nicky dame ye've a crush oan! By jings, if Ah dreampt aboot hur dial, it wid be a nightmare!"

"It's no' hur face Ah oabjec' tae," said Carole. "It's hur legs. They're merr fatter than Mick McManus's." At this witticism the young ladies were, in scientific parlance, "ferr convulsed".

Pink with rage, Eddie advanced on his sister. Before his fellow poets could stop him, he slapped Carole's face.

The police were called to the ruckus, and, to calm him down, took him for a car run – to the police office.

In court, Eddie was most contrite. "Ah think ah wiz under a emotional – er – thingmy," he explained.

Sadly, he had no rhyme of ardour to describe his feelings at having to hand over a £6 fine.

■ **Merr worser.** More worse. The tautology might be frowned upon in standard Anglish, but as an intensifier this is a highly useful term to describe the depth of Eddie's lovelorn feelings.

■ **Ferr convulsed.** Helpless with laughter. It should be pointed out that this would be a loud (let me say that again — loud) and strident sound.

Big Kitty lays Fat John oot when he refuses to lay lino

THE two small gents, friends and next door neighbours, were in revolt as they stood at the bar. "D'ye know whit Ah'm gonny tell ye?" said Fat John to Willie. "Ah'm blinkin' well fed up."

"Whirraboot?" asked Willie, removing his face from a pint pot.

"Ah've goat tae go up tae the hoose at hauf-past eight an' lay linoleum oan the kitchen flerr," said Fat John.

"Ye're no' the only wan that's fed up," Willie said darkly. "The wife wants me hame at eight o'cloke because hur sister an' hur man's comin'. An a perra hauf-wits they ur."

Deep sighs of discontent followed this dialogue.

"We'll hae anurra wan," said Willie. "Ah'm oan the bell."

Two halves and two half-pints were set before them.

They sipped in silence for a few minutes. Then – "It's comin' tae it when we canny get huvvin' a refreshment at wur leezyur oan a Friday night," said Fat John.

"Aye, thur are times when Ah wisht weemin hudny been inventit," declared Willie. "They seem tae go oot their way tae take a' the fun oota life."

"Ye're right therr," Fat John agreed. "Ye'd think we'd be able tae huv a wee refreshmint oan a Friday night wi'oot nae interference. It wid scunner ye!"

The small gents brooded over the monstrous injustice of it all.

Then, after a gloomy silence, Fat John said, "Let's have anurra." And they did. The refreshments vanished quite quickly.

"Huv we time fur annurra wan?" asked Willie.

"We'll MAKE time!" retorted his friend and neighbour.

After this order was quaffed, Fat John uttered that convivial phrase often used in Glasgow – "Wan furra road!" So they had another to fortify themselves for the arduous journey home.

Then Willie decided they should partake of "another furra road." They were doing so when bells began to ring the knell of parting drinks.

"Two haufs!" hollered Fat John above the clamour.

In the charming way of so many of the city's dispensers of strong beverages, the gentleman behind the bar intimated that he could not oblige them. "Nae merr!" he said. "The bell's went!"

"Ach, come oan, then," said Willie. "Ah suppose we'd better get back tae the wifes."

"Aw, Ah'm no' feart fur nae wife!" proclaimed Fat John. "An' Ah'll tell ye anurra thing. Ah'm layin' nae dampt lilol… ninol… waxcloath oan ony flerr the night!"

"Ye're quite right!" exclaimed Willie. "Ah'm gled we'd the sense tae … whiddycryit? … assert wursels. That's it – assert wursels! An' Ah don't gi'e a bloomin' curdie fur that frosty-faced sister-in-law o' mines, NOR that wee mug she merrit!"

This highly seditious conversation continued until they reached the landing outside their respective residences. There they shook hands and told one another what a "rerr wee session" it had been.

Suddenly the door of Fat John abode opened, and his wife, Big Kitty, appeared.

"Ya rotten wee bachle ye!" she roared. Pushing past the gents, she hammered on the opposite door and bellowed – "Haw, Annie!"

Willie's well-upholstered spouse opened her door.

"Whit the divvle happen't tae YOU?" she shouted at her husband. "Ah tell't you Clerra an' hur man wis comin' the night."

Willie faced up to her bravely, "Ah know ye did," he said. "But Ah hud a app'intment wi' Johnnie here, Ah furgoat tae tell ye Ah'd be a wee bit late."

"Good fur you, Willie!" cried Fat John admiringly. Then he turned to his own wife. "An' Ah furgoat tae tell YOU that Ah widny be layin' yer dampt waxcloath oan yer flair the night – nor ony urra night!"

"Ah'll lay ma haun' acroast your ja'!" shouted Big Kitty.

She was unable to contact the rotund gent's jaw, however, and had to content herself with giving him a thump on the cranium with her clenched fist.

"Aw, that's a libburty!" protested Willie.

His expressions of sympathy were cut short by Annie. A sharp smack across the nose from her large palm sent him reeling back into his home.

It was Big Kitty who finally ended up at the police office.

In court next day, she admitted assaulting John. "Ah'll admit Ah wiz kinna annoyed," she understated before the magistrate fined her £6.

■ **Curdie.** A small coin, perhaps a farthing (one-fourth of a penny) before they ceased to be legal tender in 1961.

■ **Whiddycryit?** What do you call it?

■ **She merrit.** She married. In Glaswegian or Anglish, both signify that a mistake was made.

Pep pills get Wee Lawrence into bather

WEE Lawrence's interest was aroused when he saw his workmate, Hughie, putting a pill in his mouth. "Goat anurra hangover?" he inquired solicitiously.

"Naw, naw, this izny an aspireen," said Hughie. "It's whit they cry a 'pep pill.' The doactur gi'ed me some fur ma nerves."

"Oh, jings, don't tell me ye're gonny turn inty a drug addic' an' a'!" exclaimed Wee Lawrence.

"Don't be daft," retorted Hughie. "Thae pills is hermless. "They're whit's known as 'non-habit-formin'. But they ferrly pep ye up – gi'e ye coanfidince. Ye waant tae try wan?"

"Aye, awright, gi'e us wan," said Wee Lawrence.

Hughie obliged and the diminutive young gent swallowed the pep pill. Anxiously he waited for it to take effect.

Suddenly his eye brightened. "Here, Ah feel rer!" he announced to Hughie. "Bags o' coanfidince! Ah widny mind tellin' that ruddy gaffer whit Ah think o' him!"

"If Ah wiz tae swally two o' thae pills Ah'd go ower an' melt the scunner," said Hughie.

As the toilers parted for the evening, Wee Lawrence said, "Gi'e us anurra o' yer pep pills."

"Sure! Erra a couple," said Hughie.

That evening, as Wee Lawrence attired himself for the dancing, he made a big decision. He would take BOTH pills. Then he would approach Pearl, the beautiful blonde he worshipped from afar.

Carefully he began to arrange his Tony Curtis curl over his forehead.

Half an hour later, he left his abode. Soon he was standing in a corner of a hostelry ordering a small ale – or, as it is known technically, a "wee strong." Lubricated by this refreshment, the two pep pills went down easily.

The young gent squared his shoulders. "Ah don't like the size o' this gless!" he called in stentorian tones to the expert who presided behind the bar. "Bring me a bigger wan – full!"

When he arrived at the dancing, Wee Lawrence felt extremely self-confident. Looking around the ladies he soon espied Pearl.

Without hesitation, he marched over to her. "Sorry tae keep ye waitin'!" he said briskly.

The young lady looked at him. On her attractive face was an expression in which utter bewilderment, icy coldness and fury were mingled.

Wee Lawrence did not seem to notice this. "Come oan," he said. "Ye don't waant tae miss ra samba, dae ye? It's ma best dance!"

Pearl shook off his hand and rose in her wrath. "Ya little soak ye!" she roared. "Ah'll 'samba' ye! Ah'll samba ma haun' acroast yer stupit-lukkin' dial!"

Wee Lawrence was not disconcerted in the least. "Ah'll show ye how tae samba!" he cried gaily.

Without further ado he embarked on a species of solo snake dance that took him out to the middle of the dancefloor.

The fact that the band was not playing at the time did not worry him at all.

A large gent connected with the management of the establishment approached him. "Heh, ye canny dae that!" protested the large gent.

"Don't be ridiculalish!" replied Wee Lawrence, engrossed in his terpsichorean gyrations. "Ah'm DAEN' it!"

"Jist a minnit, Mac," said the large gent, placing a restraining hand on his shoulder. Wee Lawrence, noting the bouncer's moustache, gave vent to a loud ejaculation of surprise.

"Oh, jings, it's Nasser!" he exclaimed. "Tryin' tae pinch anurra canaul, eh? Well, ye're no' getting' the Monklan' Canaul. An' ye're no' getting' ra Forth an' Clyde Canaul neether."

"Come oan, noo, Mac," said the large gent.

"Right, Nasser!" cried Wee Lawrence. "Come oan! Ah'll huv a go wi' ye! Ah'll learn ye tae pinch canauls!"

Gently but firmly, the pepped-up patriot was conveyed from the hall and handed over to the police.

Charged with breach of the peace, he appeared in court next morning. "Ah'd took two pills," he mumbled.

He looked anything but pepped-up when he had to stump up £1.

■ **Pep pills**. Rumours of pills with magical, or even highly aphrodisiac, qualities were much more common than the pills themselves. This story may have been a veiled warning against taking such tablets, but may also have served as an interest-alerter, depending on the reader's point of view.

■ **Nasser**. This tale is set at the time of the Suez crisis, when the charismatic (and moustachioed) Arab leader was indeed laying claim to various canals around the world.

Wee Hughie's breadboard bump after scruff comment

AMAZEMENT was writ large upon the face of Big Charlotte when she got home after visiting her sister and found her husband, Wee Hughie, seated by the fire reading a book.

"Whit's happen't?" she asked. "Ah've never saw you sittin' readin' oan a Setterday night afore. An' ye're stone cauld sober, tae! Ur ye no' weel?"

The small gent then intimated that Dougie, his usual partner in the sport of Saturday night convivialities, was the possessor of a "bad chist".

"Ah went up tae his hoose an' hud a gless o' beer jist," he added.

"Wonders'll never cease," commented his spouse. "You wi'oot a glow oan ye oan a Setterday night!"

"Aw, Ah'm no' a dampt soak a'thegither!" protested Wee Hugh. "As a matter o' fac', Dougie an' me wiz watchin' the tillyvision. He's goat BBC 2, ye know. That's a rerr programme – The Foresite Sago".

"Oh, Ah like Bruce Forsyth tae," said Big Charlotte. "Why dae they no' pit his series oan ra BBC 1 an' let a' the folk see it?"

"Ach, the Foresite Sago hus nuthin' tae dae wi' Bruce Forsyth!" Wee Hugh said scornfully. "It's a' aboot a faim'ly."

"Aw, Ah like thae faim'ly programmes!" exclaimed his wife. "Ah'm ferrly gonny miss 'Till Daith Do Us Pairt."

The small gent breathed heavily. "It's nuthin' like that programme!" he declared. "Thur nae laughs in The Foresite Sago at a'."

"It canny be much o' a programme then," said Big Charlotte.

"Look, it's a serious programme," explained the small gent. "It's a' aboot a faim'ly, whit they dae, an' who they marry an' a' that."

A sudden thought struck him. "By jings, the Foresite Sago folks izny unlike YOUR faim'ly. Only they're no' scruff."

"Who's no' scruff?" his wife wanted to know.

"The Foresites," said Wee Hugh.

"Oh, so ye're insinyatin' that ma faim'ly's scruff, ur ye?" Big Charlotte thundered.

"Ah never sayed that," said her husband.

"It's you that's sayin' it," he continued. Charlotte thought this through, trying to find a flaw in the logic.

But Hughie carried on, "Whit Ah'm tryin' tae make ye unnerstaun' is – the Foresites is like your faim'ly – a' the relatives talkin' behind wan anurra's backs an' tryin' tae dae wan anurra doon."

"Oh, so yer Foresite faim'ly's like mines, is it?" said Big Charlotte with dangerous calm.

"Well, no' exackly," Wee Hugh mused. "This faim'ly oan the TV is rich an' talks like toffs.

"Naw, Ah must admit they're a bit diff'rint fae YOUR faim'ly. Ye widny get a Foresite fella comin' up an' borrowin' yer guid suit an' a fiver aff ye an' immigratin' tae Australia."

"Oh in the name o' the wee man, ye're no oan aboot ma poor brurra again, ur ye?" roared the lady.

Her ire at this reminder of her family's questionable behaviour was so great that she felt moved to gather up a breadboard and thump her husband on the skull with it.

This ended the discussion, with Charlotte emerging the winner by way of a knockout.

However, with Hughie slow to regain consciousness, an ambulance was called, and the police came along with it.

It was obvious, by the time the case called at court, that Big Charlotte and her husband were reconciled. She deeply regretted the breadboard assault and he cheerfully assisted her to pay a £6 fine.

■ **Bad chist.** Bad chest. A bronchial complaint so severe as to limit alcohol consumption.

■ **Faim'ly.** Family. The Glasgow word is more expressive and personalised than the bland Anglish version. There are ways to pronounce "faim'ly" that can suggest a rainbow spectrum of differently slanted adjectives to describe the faim'ly – without the need to actually utter any of the adjectives.

■ **Foresite Sago.** Probably a reference to *The Forsyte Saga*, a TV drama about the world's largest gathering of toffy-nosed bauchles that ran to roughly 400 Saturday night episodes in 1967 – and then was repeated in 1968.

■ **Bruce Forsyth.** Singer, dancer, comedian, game show host . . . not previously known for his performances in period drama, although he did appear several times on *The Good Old Days*.

Skinny-legged cheuchturs in kilts get a sharp smack

THE letter that arrived at the abode of Marilyn and her sister, Christine, excited them considerably.

"It's fae yer Auntie Bette," their mother, Big Annie, had disclosed. "She's comin' tae yer Cousin Ella's weddin' an' she's bringin' the two boys wi' hur.

"It's fuffteen year since they went away tae live at the back o' beyond. Angus an' Donald'll be in their twinties noo."

"Ur they good-lookin' gents?" Christine wanted to know.

"Ah've nae idea," said Big Annie. "Ah don't think they've ever been in Glesga. Ye'll see them the morra night. They'll be at the show o' praisints at Ella's."

"Oh, here, if they're hauf-daisint-lookin' we'll get them tae lumbur us tae the dancin'!" cried Marilyn.

But, at the show of presents the following evening, the sisters' enthusiasm vanished as soon as they met their cousins, Angus and Donald.

The young gents were the reverse of the Mod type. They were on the stubby side, and they wore the kilt. As soon as they could, Marilyn and Christine retired to a corner.

"Oh, whit a dampt let-doon!" Marilyn whispered fiercely. "They're jist a coupla cheuchtur chumps! Wid ye look at thur wee skinny legs!"

It's thur faces that's the worst," whispered back Christine. "They're sittin' therr lookin' like a perra sheepdugs waitin' fur a bone."

Their acidulous discourse was cut short by the hearty voice of their Auntie Bette. "Here you young anes!" she cried in her rustic patois. "You shouldna be settin' aboot here wi' us auld fowk! Can you laddies no' tak' yer kizzens oot and aboot for a walk doon the hedgerows?"

"Loash, mither, that's a beezer idea!" cried Angus. "Donald an' me dinna ken this toon ava, though. Maybe the lassies could show us the sichts."

"Big deal!" growled Christine as she and her sister prepared to go out on their unwanted date.

For nearly an hour the quartet wandered along various nearby streets.

The young ladies were silent for the most part. But their country cousins had plenty to say. "Ah dinna think Ah could stey in the toon," Angus declared. "Sic a lot o' motor cars and buses! The air's fu' o' fumes. Ah feel it in ma throat."

"Mibbe a gless o' somethin' wid help it," said Marilyn. "Thur a nice wee coacktail lounge in the nixt street. "We could go in an' huv a …"

"Oh, Angus an' me never gang intil sich places!" Donald told her. "Ye'll never catch us wi' a glawss in oor hauns! We're guid members o' The Kirk an' teetotallers, ye ken."

At that Donald drew out his pocket watch. "Loash me!" he cried. "It's very near haun' ten o'clock! It's time we were makkin' tracks back til the hoose!"

"Gee whizz ye're richt!" exclaimed Angus. "The fowks'll be getting' worried aboot us. Mither'll be thinkin' we've eloped wi' the lassies!"

The lads har-har-hawed at this hilarious line.

"Ah'd as soon elope wi' Alf Garnett," muttered Christine to Marilyn. "In fac', Ah canny stick this coupla foosty cheuchturs a minute longer. Let's beat it alang tae the late-night rave-up at the Midden Club."

The kilted gents were amazed and indignant at this notion. "There's yer smart city anes for ye!" complained Donald to his brother. "Ye tak' them fur a walk an' they want to rin awa' tae some den o' inquitnity."

"Ach, shut yer stupit wee face, ya little skinflint ye!" screeched Christine, giving Donald a sharp smack on the face.

A particularly noisy row ensued.

The leading light in this fracas, Christine, was taken into custody on a breach of the peace charge.

"Ach, it wiz just a family argymint, atween cousins," she insisted in court.

The magistrate did not regard this as a mitigating factor and a howl of dismay went up from Christine when he fined her £4.

■ **Show o' praisints.** Show of presents. A quaint and quite strange pre-wedding ritual at which various members of a family would gather to view, and fiercely criticise, a couple's wedding gifts.

■ **Cheuchtur.** Country person. An insult. People from outwith Glasgow are all strange.

■ **Loash!** It is anybody's guess what this means. It is clearly foreign talk.

Tommy scents trouble after perfume bottle mix-up

IN preparation for his date with the beauteous Isa, Tommy was spending considerable time and trouble on his toilette.

After shaving, he picked up a small bottle from the bathroom shelf and rubbed fully half the contents into his smooth chin and cheeks.

A few minutes later, when he was dressed and smoothing down the long points of his red and purple collar in front of the kitchen looking glass, he became aware of the sound of sniffling nearby.

It came from his sister, Norma. "Aw, hivvins, don't tell me you've goat the snuffles again!" he said. "Try an' keep yer flu germs tae yersel', wull ye?"

But Norma sniffed on. Suddenly she burst out with "That's ma guid perfume ye've goat oan!"

And she scurried off to examine the bottle in the bathroom.

In a few seconds she was back, brandishing the small bottle aloft. "Hauf o' it's away!" she cried with great anguish. "Ye've slabber't ma perfume that Ah paid a poun' fur oan yer ugly big gub!"

"Well, Ah thought it wiz efter-shave lotion," said her brother. "Ye shouldny leave it lyin' aboot."

"Maw, maw, he's went an' stole hauf ma perfume!" wailed the young lady.

The matriarch of the family, Big Gracie, laid aside her newspaper. "'Sup?" she inquired.

Norma reiterated her complaint.

"Well, whit kin AH dae aboot it?" asked Tommy.

Big Gracie then used her maternal wisdom to smooth out the trouble. "Gi'e hur ten boab fur that perfume ye've pinched or Ah'll knoack the heid aff ye," she intoned.

Tommy knew better than to refuse and handed the note to his sister.

"That's the bloomin' limit!" he grumbled. "Hauf a quid fur rubbin' a wee drap stuff oan ma face!"

He was still smarting with what he considered a grave injustice when he went off to meet Isa.

As they trudged through the wind and rain to the dancing, the young lady was unaware her swain was heavily perfumed.

But the heat of the small hall brought out the full bouquet of the scent.

"In the name o' hivvins, whit's that smell?" asked Isa, apparently no connoisseur of the products of the Paris perfume manufacturers. "Is it YOU it's comin' fae? Whitizzit?"

"Is it the perfume ye smell?" asked Tommy apprehensively. The young lady looked at him amazed.

"Perfume?" she echoed. "Oh, that's chronic! It's gi'en me a headache."

"Ah peyed ten boab fur it," growled Tommy.

"Ye mean ye went inty a shope an' spent ten shillins oan a boattle o' perfume?" asked Isa. "Noo Ah've heard everythin'! Ah don't mind yer long herr. But PERFUME! Ye'll be cerryin' a haun'bag nixt!"

"It's ma sister's perfume," growled the young gent.

Isa was bewildered. "Don't tell me ye sherr a boattle o' perfume wi' yer sister!" she exclaimed. "Does she gi'e ye a shot o' hur curlers tae?"

At this quaint conceit she burst into raucous laughter.

On top of his ten shilling loss, and his embarrassment at smelling like a peony, Tommy found this difficult to endure.

He put a sudden end to her noisy mirth by slapping her across the mouth.

Three seconds later the fragrant gent was being quickly escorted outside, and soon he was passed on to the custody of the police.

"Ah never done nuthin' like that afore," he said in court the next day.

The magistrate took a lenient view and let him off with a £5 fine.

■ **Whitizzit?** What is it? Note the rapier-like, get-straight-to-the-point quality of Isa's inquiry. This is a piercing phrase that, in its simplicity and decisiveness, will be the envy of interviewers and interrogators across the land. This isn't merely language, it is art given sound.

■ **Slabber't.** Slabbered. The Anglish equivalent stays quite close to the sound of the Glaswegian original in this instance, but evokes a less vivid impression of splatteryness and splashiness.

■ **Ye'll be cerryin' a haun'bag nixt!** The concept of a man-bag was still some years distant.

Kerry-on when Wee George sneaks in a kerry-oot

THE fact that Ronnie, her next-door neighbour, went to work carrying a briefcase impressed Big Jean tremendously.

She told her husband, Wee George, about it. "You should get wan," she said. The small gent looked up at her balefully. "Whit the divvle wid Ah waant wi' a briefcase?" he asked. "It's sheer swank. That fella next door jist kerries his piece in it."

"It looks well," contended Big Jean. "It wid gi'e ye a toucha class. An', by jings, ye could dae wi' THAT!"

Her husband made a disparaging noise and set off for the day's toil. On his way home in the evening, he dropped in at the local hostelry for a refreshment. There, at the bar, stood Ronnie complete with briefcase.

"Whit the heck d'ye kerry that thing aboot wi' ye fur?" Wee George asked him scornfully. "Don't tell me ye've jine't MI5 an' ye're totin' secret doacuments aboot wi' ye."

Ronnie looked at him with 007-like mysteriousness. "Ye don't gerrit," he said. He looked over his shoulder and lowered his voice. "This briefcase," he said. "Ah take ma sandwidges tae the work right anough. But it's reely fur a fly kerry-oot."

"Ah'm no wi' ye at a'," said Wee George. "How d'ye mean?"

Ronnie explained. "It's the wife, ye see," he revealed. "She'd fly aff the haun'le if Ah came in wi' a paper bag wi' cans o' beer in it. So Ah smuggle it in in this briefcase an' when she goes oot tae the bingo Ah kin sit back and huv a pint or two tae masel'."

"Ah see," said the small gent, pondering the information. "That's no' a bad idea!" he exclaimed. "Ma missus aye gi'es me a dirty look if Ah as much as bring in a wee boattle o' stout."

He watched admiringly as Ronnie bought several cans of beer and stowed them in his briefcase.

"By crivvins, it's like huvvin' yer ain private cellar!" enthused Wee George. "Aw Ah'm gonny huv a go at this caper!"

He equipped himself with a capacious briefcase forthwith.

"It's a right big yin," commented Big Jean, "Ah'll be able tae get the messidges inty it oan a Setterday."

That evening, George followed Ronnie's example and loaded his briefcase with four cans and a quarter bottle of whisky.

As soon as he got into the house he slipped it into the lobby press.

"Noo, don't you be sneakin' oot tae the coarnur shope when Ah'm alang seein' ma maw the night," Big Jean warned.

"Ah wizny thinkin' o' daen' nae sich thing!" said her husband indignantly.

Impatiently he awaited his wife's departure for the abode of her mother. "It'll no' be worth gaun' if ye don't go soon," he said.

"Well, you dry thae dishes an' Ah'll get away," snapped back the lady, throwing a dishcloth to him.

"Well, Ah'm away," she said at last and left the house.

Her husband was making his way, with gleeful anticipation, to the lobby press when the doorbell rang.

"It's me," said Big Jean when he opened the door. "Ah furgoat tae take ma knittin'." She went to the lobby press and procured the half-finished jumper, the wool, and needles.

"Wherr a bit paper tae pit it in?" she muttered. Then she had a thought. "Oh, Ah'll kerry it in that briefcase o' yours."

"Naw! Naw!" cried her husband. "Ye'll waste it! The...the knittin' needles'll stick inty it!"

"Whit ur ye talkin' aboot?" asked the large lady as she picked up the briefcase. There was a clanking sound from within.

She quickly unzipped it. "Ya rotten wee fly man ye!" she cried. "A load o' booze planked away so's ye could ha'e a wee perty tae yersel' while Ah wiz oot!"

"Noo wait a meenit –" began Wee George.

"So THAT'S why ye goat a briefcase?" bellowed the lady. "Well, Ah'm gonny lock that beer and whisky in ma display cabinet, an' Ah'm takin' awa' the key!"

"Naw!" shouted her husband, making a grab for the briefcase.

Big Jean extracted a tin and persuaded him to desist by banging it on his countenance.

The contretemps led to the large lady's appearance in court on an assault charge. "Ah'll 'briefcase' the wee nyuck!" she muttered darkly as she paid her £5 fine.

■ **Swank**. The act of appearing to have ideas above your station. The details of putting on "swank" would vary from person to person, but would be very obvious to neighbours or indeed any observers.

■ **His piece**. His sandwiches/lunch/snack.

■ **A wee boattle o' stout in ma poackit**. There is no use denying it, the Glasgow of the 1950s and '60s had a strong drinking culture. That folk took a drink was a universally-accepted and simple fact of life. Cheers, here's tae ye.

Wee Daisy's Dutch courage sparks a tenement feud

IT'S surprising how some women become fearless when they're in convivial company.

Normally, Wee Daisy had hardly a word to say. But when she accompanied a few lady friends to the sitting room of the corner shop and had a few snifters, she felt as brave as a lion.

"Come oan an' we'll go back tae the street an' Ah'll gie that big midden a right good hidin'," she said.

The other ladies did not need to ask the identity of the person who, in Daisy's opinion, was a large rubbish pit. It could only be Big Annie. That very morning, Big Annie had termed Wee Daisy a "stupit wee heidcase".

"Come oan," Wee Daisy urged the ladies in the hostelry sitting-room. "Ah'll dae the talkin'. Ah'll tell hur a few things that'll mak hur sit up."

So, led by the diminutive heroine, the company made their way to the street. They halted just below Big Annie's window.

Wee Daisy stepped forward, raised her head and screeched at the window – "Heh, ya big fat hoatch, come doon noo an' say whit ye sayed tae me this mornin'."

Big Annie, seated with her husband Hughie at the kitchen table taking tea, was quite unaware that she was being invited to make a personal appearance.

"Who's that shoutin the odds doon therr?" asked Hughie.

"Ach, it's jist some drunk wumman," said his wife.

"Lizzie Thingmy like anough. Hur man hud a guid win at the dugs las' night."

Again the voice floated up from the street. "Ah, ye're feart tae show yer ugly big dial!" yelled Wee Daisy. "Rotten big twister, that's whit ye ur!"

"Who the divvle is it?" said Big Annie, rising and going to the window. Then she saw Wee Daisy.

A screech of hate escaped Daisy when she saw her large enemy staring down at her.

"Therr she's!" she cried. "Therr's the wumman that's a disgrace tae the tinnymint."

Big Annie kept her temper. She raised her window, looked down at Daisy for a moment, then called, "Ye're puggle't. Awa' inty yer dirty wee hoose an' sleep it aff."

Wee Daisy, enraged beyond measure by this assessment of her state of sobriety and domestic cleanliness, shook her fist. "Lazy big loafer, that's whit ye ur," she howled.

Then she proceeded to outline the large lady's failings to her companions. "She'll no' waash doon the sterr an' she'll no' dae a waashin' unless therr's somebody in the waash-hoose she wants tae spite!" declared the small lady.

"In fac', she hates the sight o' watter!"

Big Anne listened to these allegations with commendable aplomb. "Therr's ladylike talk fur ye," she remarked to her husband. "Ye know, if ma coarns wizny gi'en me gyp, Ah'd go doon therr an' belt the gub aff that wee scunner."

"Ach, close the windae an' doan't boather wi' hur," said her husband in some alarm. "The Black Maria'll be here tae lift hur if she cerries oan ony longer."

Big Annie heeded him not. In fact, she raised the window a full six inches more. Then she popped her head out and called down to Wee Daisy – "Aaach, shut yer face, ya wee horror."

"Try an' furget ye're feart o' watter an' waash YOUR face," requested Wee Daisy, marching forward so that her angry, contorted countenance was upraised right beneath the window.

It was what the large lady had hoped for – a perfect target.

With a minimum of arm movement, she emptied the triangular receptacle containing tea leaves and potato peelings into the basin of dishwater in the sink over which she was leaning.

"Seein' you're that fond o' watter, here's some fur ye," called Big Annie, emptying the basin quickly.

With a wild shriek, Wee Daisy tried to dodge the sheet of water. In vain.

A split second later, she stood soaked to the skin, festooned with potato peelings, and yelling with chagrin in an ear-damagingly loud manner.

Then the police arrived and Wee Daisy and Big Annie were booked for breach of the peace.

"She stertit it a'" said the large lady, recounting the whole story in court the next day.

Daisy had nothing to say. She wept when she was fined £2. Big Annie got off with a stern warning.

■ **Hoatch.** A large, ungainly or untidy woman.

■ **She'll no' waash doon the sterr.** On a rota basis, the occupants of every flat in a tenement would take turns to wash, or at least brush out, the communal stairwell. Failure to do this, or a lacklustre effort, resulted in strong feelings.

Rita v. Big Roberta in Okeydokey showdown

THE patrons of the Okeydokey Club were intrigued by the notice outside the noted dance resort.

"Do not miss Roberta!" It read. "Sensational artiste! Usual admission!" The identity of Roberta was not disclosed until, heralded by a dramatic fanfare from Fred and his Band of Boogie Woogie Bachles, Wee Andy M.C. appeared.

"Ladies and gentlemens!" asked the Master of Ceremonies. "What has been on the lips of all youse ones here tonight?"

"The necks o' screwtaps an' awfy wee wineglasses," came the prompt answer from an all-too-familiar voice.

The benign smile vanished from Wee Andy's face when he saw that Rita the Critic was once again present.

"Madam," he said, "I was not making no reference to no imbibulating activities that may have been indulged in by various sundry patrons. Furdermore, kindly cease for to puncturate my words with your unrevelant remarks."

Rita was silenced by this rebuke. Temporarily.

The stern look on Wee Andy's face was replaced by a smile as he continued his announcement. "I do not propose for to withhold the identify of Roberta from you no longer," he said.

"Allow me for to now introduce to you one of the most foremostest lady saxophonists in our city – Roberta!"

The Boog-Woogie Bachles burst into a few bars of the Billy May classic *Fat Man Boogie*. This was answered by a collection of loud rasping saxophone notes.

Then Roberta, an intimidatingly large girl in black velvet jeans and a violent rose-coloured sweater, lumbered smilingly on to the band platform. She carried a gilt saxophone.

"Welcome to our lady virtuotosio of the saxapaphone!" cried the Master of Ceremonies. "Anurra of my very own discoveries!"

"Whaur did ye discover hur – under a stane? Big stane, mind." Rita observed. Fortunately, Roberta was conferring with Fred and the Bachles and did not hear the remark.

After a brief glare at Rita, Wee Andy turned to his discovery Roberta and inquired: "And what are you going to give us?"

"Serr eardrums," suggested Rita.

"Aw, Ah don't know that number," said Big Roberta, whose accent revealed her place of domicile was probably somewhat removed from the jazz palaces of New Orleans. She continued, "But I would like to play for youse a speshul favourite of mines – Flaminago."

Without further ado, the orchestra struck up and, presently, Roberta launched into her solo.

The tempo was very slow. As the young lady blew, and sweated freely, she closed her eyes and looked agonised.

At one juncture, as she paused for breath, Rita's voice was heard, loud and clear. "She luks as if she hud a pain in hur big peeny," she observed.

When the number ended, Wee Andy led the applause. "That was Flamingio," he said, holding out his arm in salute to the now breathless Roberta.

"It soundit like a turkey gettin' its heid choapped aff," said Rita.

Roberta rose to the challenge. "Somebody's axin' fur a clout oan the crust!" she shrilled. "An' they're gonny gerrit!"

"Please!" entreated the Master of Ceremonies, holding up a hand in an effort to dissuade Roberta from taking matters further. "Allow me for to handle the situation heres. I shall make very ensure that there is not no furder interruptions."

But his plea was in vain as the light of battle had been kindled in Roberta's eye. The enraged sax blower, whose wrestler-shouldered height and width made her an opponent of some seriousness, leaped from the band platform and rushed at Rita.

The Critic was not perturbed. She had seen this before. At the last moment she pivoted on one high heel, sidestepped the onrushing large lady like a matador, and dealt a resounding slap across the face of the virtuoso as she blundered by.

"This is most outrageful!" protested Wee Andy.

Rita aimed a blow at him. But Andy had also seen this before. And as Rita's fist swung he managed simultaneously to duck and emit his now famous low emergency whistle. The henchmen quickly helped Rita along her well-trodden path to the door.

In court next day, she was still seething. "Fined a coupla quid!" she ejaculated. "An' Ah never even goat a decent belt at him!"

■ **Rita**. With some sadness, this will be the last appearance of Rita on these pages. She has dealt her last slap, swung her last haymaker. Her modus operandi has become somewhat predictable, with even the ever optimistic Wee Andy M.C. issuing tired warnings as to her conduct. However, the world of entertainment owes Rita a huge debt. Her withering assessment skills were clearly the blueprint for all TV talent show "bad guy" judges of the future – though none ever did quite have her talent for violence. Farewell, Rita the Critic.

Rena wrecks Bob's romantic marriage proposal

IT could hardly be said that Bob was the most articulate of young gents. Consequently, he viewed the prospect of asking Rena to marry him with considerable trepidation.

But he was determined to do the deed when they went to the discotheque in the evening.

It was perhaps unfortunate that she was not in the best of tempers when he met her aff the bus.

"Whit a dampt awfy day Ah've hud in the shope!" she complained. "That manager laddie disnae ken nane whit he's daen. Sends abody a'where and nane of them wi' a clue whit tae dae.

"An' tae make matters worser Ah tripped ower a big bag o' totties an' hit ma big toe oan the side o' the counter."

"Ye'll feel merr better when ye get a cuppa coaffy in the disco," said Bob tenderly.

"Whit's the use o' gaun' therr?" the young lady wanted to know. "Ah'll no' be able tae dance wi' ma serr fit."

"Well … er … Ah've a special reason fur waantin' tae go therr," said her swain, thinking of the dim romantic lighting in the discotheque.

Mystified, the young lady let herself be talked into accompanying him to the venue.

"Aw, Ah see why ye've brung me here," she said as they sat at a table. "They've goat a chinge o' records at last. Mind you, the new wans are bloomin' lousy, tae… Oh ma big toe's loupin' like the divvle!"

It was hardly the most convivial atmosphere for a marriage proposal.

But Bob was determined to see his mission through. "Err… look… err… thur somethin' Ah waant tae ask ye," he mumbled. "D'ye know whit it is?"

"Aye! An' Ah'm no' loaning ye ANURRA quid!" came the sharp response. "Whit did ye dae wi' the wancer Ah loaned ye oan Friday therr? "Ma mithir aye sayed tae look oot fur ye were a fly ane."

"Naw, naw. Wait a minnut!" cried Bob in the beginnings

of desperation at his romantic intentions being so terribly misunderstood (and worried that he might be asked to pay back the £1). "Whit Ah'm tryin' tae say is – whit about us yins getting' spliced?"

There was no prim Victorian-style reaction from Rena, no coy turning of the head, no fluttered eyelash with a murmured "Oh! This is so sudden!"

"Ya must be aff yer ruddy roacker!" she exploded. "Whit makes ye think Ah'd ever think o' marryin' YOU?"

"Well Ah've been takin' ye oot fur nearly a month noo," Bob pointed out.

"Ye mean Ah've been takin' YOU oot!" stated Rena. "Every time we've went tae the dancin' ye've tapped me fur a loan. Ye seem tae think Ah'm a tap-dancer."

Bob realised that he might never achieve domestic bliss with Rena.

He rose and looked down at her coldly. "Ach ya crabbit bizzim ye!" he exclaimed. "Ah'd like tae give ye a tap oan yer crusty-lookin' dial!"

So saying, the rejected paramour strode from the discotheque.

A few minutes later he was walking along the pavement when he felt a hefty crack on his skull and everything went blank.

Rena, stung by his "crust" threat, had stolen up behind and vented her wrath with the hefty wooden handle of her umbrella.

She showed little remorse when she appeared next day in court on an assault charge.

"The scunner's skull wizny as thick as Ah thought it wiz," she muttered as she paid her £7 fine.

The marriage didn't happen.

■ **Crabbit**. Bad tempered.

■ **Totties**. Potatoes.

■ **Loupin**. Infested with vermin.

■ **Whit about us yins getting' spliced?** A proposal of marriage is a rare thing in these police court stories, as is the description of an assault carried out from behind in a sneak manner. This was the seventies, and the times they were a-changing.

Sultry Susan cuts loose on impatient punter

THE state of agitation Boab was in gave his friend, Sammy, cause for concern when they met in the street.

"Whissa marra?" inquired the latter. "Huz the wife ran aff wi' the ludger?"

"Worser'n that!" Boab revealed. "Ah've goat a good thing fur the three-thirty an' Ah canny find a phone tae pit oan a bet wi' the bookie! They're a' broke up."

"Thur a phone boax workin' doon therr at the bus terminus," Sammy old him.

Boab hurried on. When he arrived at the thankfully unvandalised phone box, however, he was dismayed to find that Susan, a comely blonde who lived in the neighbourhood, was in possession. She was in animated telephonic badinage with one of her suitors.

Thanks to a missing pane of glass, Boab heard her uttering such coy statements as – "Oh, Alfie, ye shouldny say them kinna things!... Of course Ah dae, silly!... Oh ye do nutt!... Oh Ah don't believe ye, Alfie!... D'ye REELLY think Ah look like Julie Ege?"

"Tell yer pal Alfie tae get aff the line or Ah'll scatter him," shouted Boab. "Ah've a bet tae pit oan an' Ahm no' gonny manidge it in time if him an' you keeps oan bletherin yer stupit chaff!"

So saying, the desperate racing enthusiast opened the door of the phone box and snatched at the receiver.

"It's wan o' thae vandals that's tryin' tae get in an' wreck the phone, Alfie," she explained to her boy friend.

A second later Boab gave a cry of pain. The young lady had jabbed the receiver against his nose.

Clutching his damaged organ, he staggered back. Susan calmly closed the door and resumed her conversation.

"Oh, ye've pit anurra two pence in?" she said, highly flattered. "Wherr wiz we? Oh, aye, ye wiz sayin' Ah looked like – "

"Ah'm gonny get the polis tae you!" cried Boab, wrenching open the door of the phone box.

"Aw, here it's again," sighed the damsel. "Excuse me anurra saicint, Alfie."

This time, the toe of her jackboot caught Boab flush on the shin. He was forced to retire from the fray again, holding his leg and hopping about on one foot.

Susan went on with her conversation with Alfie, but Boab's language, as he yowled in pain and kept up his moans at the need to speak to a turf accountant, was, to put it mildly, somewhat vigorous.

A lady who regularly took tea with the minister's wife, who was passing by, took exception to this manner of talk. She hurried on and was soon lodging her objections to this bad language to the police.

Two constables went to the phone box and found Boab still vociferating and still trying to gain entrance. Susan was still ignoring him.

Boab was summarily removed and charged with a breach of the peace.

In court he was much quieter, but still extremely bitter. "Hivvins, Ah get ma nose near took aff me, an' ma leg aboot broke an' Ah end up here!" he protested as he limped into court.

"It's no' ferr!" he added as he paid his £4 fine.

■ **The toe of her jackboot.** Susan is clearly another Glasgow lady well-practiced in close-order combat, able to deal out "reducers" to anyone who crosses her. Her casual, almost care-free, demeanour while delivering crippling blows to a larger opponent just adds to her superhuman aura. She is another example of a self-possessed, ultra-capable Glasgow woman. There is little sign, throughout this entire book, of women being unable to speak up for themselves or to act on their own volition. The gender equality revolution came quicker and easier to Glasgow womanhood than most other communities around the world. Cross a Glasgow woman at your peril!

■ **Julie Ege.** Norwegian glamour model and actress who appeared in 1969 Bond film *On Her Majesty's Secret Service*. Her prowess as a fighter with phone handsets and/or jackboots as weapons is unknown, though she isn't thought to have ever lived in Glasgow.

■ **Language somewhat vigorous.** This oblique reference is a rare acknowledgment that some of the words used in these tales might be euphemised. However, swearing was, perhaps surprisingly, much rarer in those far-off days. Even the drunkest, durtiest scunner would be unlikely to use intemperate language in public.

Susan sinks a Doric dance-hall dreamboat

SUSAN surveyed herself in the looking-glass, examining her long, straight blonde hair critically and her short, black, sack-like dress.

Then she sighed. "Y'see, ma trouble is – Ah reckon Ah've outgrew Glesca."

"How rat?" asked her friend, Jane, smearing almost-white lipstick on her mouth.

Susan explained. "Well, Ah'd really like tae live doon in Chelsea," she said. "London, ye know. That's whaur a' the trendsetters, an' that, is.

"Ah mean, look at the fellas here, for instince. They're no' with-it in thur dress, an' they don't huv nae smart coanvursation like the London fellas."

They were still discussing the regrettable lack of male trendsetters in Glasgow when they arrived at the small dance hall they frequented.

"Same as usual," commented Susan with a grimace of distaste. "They're a' weans or dafties. There's nutt a with-it fella in the lot."

"Hey, hey!" said Jane excitely. "Wait a minnit. Whit aboot that fella staunnin' at the coaffy bar therr? By jings, he looks like a Chelsea joab a' right! Thur a touch o' the Engelbert Humperdincks aboot him."

Susan noted the lightweight mauve suit, the flower-patterned shirt with ultra high collar, and the broad tie with multi-coloured stars on it.

"Aye. He's deffynately no' fae Glesca!" she concluded considerably impressed with the looks of the fellow.

The with-it gent caught her eye, strolled over and, with a charming new-world courtesy, indicated to Susan that he would like to dance with her.

"Right?" he said with a curt nod.

The trend-setting damsel preceded him to the dance floor. "Now Ah know you're no' fae Glesca, ur ye!" she said excitedly when he caught up with her. "Huv ye jist arrived fae London? Or Chickyago?"

She stopped dancing and recoiled in dismay when the

young gent replied to her question. "Ah'm chust a loon fae up Peetercooter wiy, min," he revealed, "Fit made ye thenk Ah heelt fae London or onyplace?"

"Oh in the name o' the wee man. A dampt furriner!" gasped the young lady.

"Look mister, Ah've made a mistake! Ah thought ye wiz a with-it man fae Chelsea."

"Na, Aw'm an orraman doon fae Aiberdeen wiy," her partner explained. "Hae ye nivvir heard of Peetercooter, like?

"Ah'm bidin' wi' ma guid sister oan a ferm near hand tae the toon here, ye see. Ah thocht Ah'd hev a looksee at the Glasgae quinies ower this wiy."

"Aye, aye, okay," interrupted Susan, barely understanding a word of what he'd said. "Oh, umm, ye'll huv tae excuse me. Ma pal's sittin' by herself. . ."

"Dinna fash yersel', quine, yer freen can bide hursel fir a wee bitty." said the ornate orraman. "Bide up an Aw'll pit ye through your paces!"

"NAW!" cried Jane, who had rushed to her friend's assistance.

"Come on, noo!" said the would-be dance partner restraining Susan by the arm with the practised controlling touch of an experienced cattleman.

"Aw beetle aff, ya dampt impositer ye!" screeched Susan. And she gave the Doric gent a hearty thump on the chest then a slap on the face.

Both young ladies, protesting vociferously, were hustled from the hall and handed over to the police.

Jane was allowed away without charge, but Susan was indignant when she appeared in court charged with breach of the peace.

"That big fermin lout wiz pesterin' me!" she exclaimed. "Ah HUD tae gie him a scud oan the face!"

She groaned when the magistrate fined her £2.

■ **Orraman**. Farm-hand, ordinary worker.

■ **Weans**. Wee 'ane. Wee one. Small one. Children.

■ **Dampt furriner**. Anyone from outwith Glasgow was a damned foreigner.

■ **Dinna fash yersel'**. Unintelligible foreign talk that could mean anything. No one knows. These ridiculous sounding words, with their odd spellings, prove that Glaswegian is the one true language. People who dinnae understand the patter dinnae know nane.

Thanks to . . .

. . . the various bachles, middens and cheuchters who gave their invaluable help with this book.

Chloe Copland.
David Powell
Barry Sullivan.
Gill Martin.
Sylwia Jackowska.
Jacqui Hunter.
Craig Houston.
Leon Strachan.
James Kirk.
Dawn Donaghey.
Scott Binnie.
Mike Rankin.
Carole Finan.
Rebecca Finan.
Lewis Finan.
Maggie Dun.
Fraser T. Ogilvie.
The city of Glasgow and everyone who ever lived there.

I don't know where I'd be without you all.
Las Vegas, probably.

Steve Finan 2020

If you liked this book, you'll also enjoy these books...